Criminal Justice
Recent Scholarship

Edited by
Marilyn McShane and Frank P. Williams III

A Series from LFB Scholarly

Peer Reporting of Unethical Police Behavior

Vedat Kargin

LFB Scholarly Publishing LLC
El Paso 2011

Copyright © 2011 by LFB Scholarly Publishing LLC

All rights reserved.

Library of Congress Cataloging-in-Publication Data

Kargin, Vedat, 1973-
  Peer reporting of unethical police behavior / Vedat Kargin.
    p. cm.
  Includes bibliographical references and index.
  ISBN 978-1-59332-448-3 (hardcover : alk. paper)
  1. Police--Pennsylvania--Philadelphia. 2. Peer review--Pennsylvania--Philadelphia. 3. Police-community relations--Pennsylvania--Philadelphia. 4. Police misconduct--Pennsylvania--Philadelphia. 5. Police discretion--Pennsylvania--Philadelphia. I. Title.
  HV7571.P4K37 2010
  363.2'2--dc22
                                      2010039290

ISBN 978-1-59332-448-3

Printed on acid-free 250-year-life paper.

Manufactured in the United States of America.

Dedication

To my wife, Hande, and our beloved children, Meryem, Yusuf, and Mustafa.

Contents

Acknowledgements ix

CHAPTER ONE
Introduction 1

CHAPTER TWO
Theories of Ethical Decision Making 9

CHAPTER THREE
Factors Associated With Peer Reporting 37

CHAPTER FOUR
Roadmap to Research 79

CHAPTER FIVE
Empirical Findings 101

CHAPTER SIX
Discussion and Implications 125

Appendices 143

References 153

Index 171

Acknowledgements

I would like to acknowledge several individuals and organizations for their support and contributions to this book. First, I would like to thank Dr. Alida V. Merlo, who has provided invaluable advice and direction to complete this work. I want to thank Dr. Willard T. Austin, Dr. Daniel R. Lee, and Dr. John A. Lewis for their assistance and constructive feedback in the process of writing this book.

I am in great debt to my wife, daughter, and son for their love, patience, and indulgence during my stay in the U.S. They had to bear a lot but have never withheld their patience, support, and love from during our stay in the U.S. Our son, Mustafa, the newest addition to our family, has doubled our excitement and joy at the end of our time in the U.S.

I would also like to acknowledge the Turkish Government, the Turkish National Police, and the Turkish taxpayers who provided economic support throughout my stay in the U.S.

CHAPTER 1
INTRODUCTION

This book examines police officers' ethical decision making with regard to reporting a peer's unethical behaviors within an organization. Peer reporting is a special type of ethical decision making behavior (Barnett, Bass, & Brown, 1996; Trevino & Victor, 1992), and it has been one of the positive outcome behaviors investigated in the ethical decision making literature (Trevino et al., 2006). One of the purposes of this book is to develop an ethical decision making model for the investigation of police officers' peer reporting decision. A second one is to test the model and understand what influences police officers' peer reporting decision.

On a theoretical level, this book examines police officers' ethical decision making processes integrating major ethical decision making theoretical models proposed in the area of ethical decision making. Rest's (1984) "four component model" which explains individual ethical decision making processes is incorporated along with Trevino's (1986) "person-situation interactionist" model and Jones' (1991) "issue-contingent model." Thus, police officers' ethical decision making within a police department is investigated by incorporating individual level variables, organizational level variables, and issue-related variables drawn from these models. This approach also integrates the two most common approaches identified in the literature in the examination of police unethical behavior: the individual level approach and the more contemporary organizational/occupational approach (Klockars et al., 2004).

From a practical perspective, the behavior examined, peer reporting, has significant implications for police organizations and administrators to control unethical practices of police officers within organization. As such, peer reporting of unethical behavior is suggested as a potential supplementary control mechanism to cope with employees' unethical behavior within organizations (Trevino & Victor, 1992). Therefore, this book informs police administrators about the factors and the extent of their influence on police officers' peer reporting decisions. By knowing both the factors and the extent of their influence on police officers' peer reporting decisions, police administrators will have valuable information that will enable them to improve conditions (i.e., individual or organizational) that might lead to unethical behaviors and to enhance their efforts to reduce future unethical behaviors by the members of the organization.

The Problem

Police officers are empowered to use force, intervene in the affairs of the citizenry, and remove citizens' constitutional rights under certain conditions (Barker, 2006; Caldero & Crank, 2004). The decisions and behaviors of police have tremendous consequences on the quality of police service and the well-being of society (Sherman, 1978), especially with respect to public confidence in the police (Goldstein, 1975). Felkenes (1987) argues that the quality of police work and service and the administering of police procedures depend on how the police handle situations involving ethical problems and dilemmas that they encounter in their daily activities. Therefore, the importance of ethical decision making and ethical behavior in police work cannot be underestimated.

On the other hand, police work often involves many complex and emergent issues about which police officers have to make decisions. In performing routine duties, police come in close contact with citizens; and, in most instances, work in environments with low supervision where there are opportunities for unethical behavior (Barker, 2006; Goldstein, 1975; Sherman, 1982). The nature of the police occupation also involves the discretionary use of power and authority, the existence of and widespread opportunities and temptations conducive to unethical behavior, and loyalty to colleagues, commonly referred to as the "code of silence" or the "blue curtain" (Barker, 2006; Felkenes, 1987; Ivkovic, 2003; Law Enforcement report, 1998; Sherman, 1982). These features of police work are the sources of unethical practices of police personnel according to a number of researchers (Barker, 1977; Caldero & Crank, 2004; Kleinig, 1996; Klockars, Ivkovic, Haberfeld, Harver, 2000; Sherman, 1978, 1985; Skolnick, 2002).

Unethical practices of police personnel, especially in the form of police corruption have had a long history, virtually beginning with the early foundations of police departments (Barker, 2006; Barker & Carter, 1994; Goldstein, 1975). Although there are no data about actual incidences of police corruption, Sherman (1985) and Ivkovic (2003) contend that corruption always is possible where there are police.

The history of controlling and preventing police unethical behavior shows that a variety of mechanisms have been developed and implemented within police organizations, such as a police code of ethics, Internal Affairs Units, Early Intervention Systems, police auditors, and citizen oversight (Walker, 2005). However, police unethical behaviors (i.e., excessive force, corruption, and race discrimination) "might appear to be as prevalent and serious today as they were 40 years earlier" (Walker, 2005, p. 11). Among the reasons, the "code of silence" is considered to be the biggest obstacle in identifying and investigating the unethical practices of police personnel by many academicians (i.e., Ivkovic, 2003; Kleinig, 1996; Klockars, Ivkovic, & Haberfeld, 2004; Skolnick, 2002; Westmarland, 2005).

The code is an unwritten rule and refers to loyalty and brotherhood among police personnel that informally prohibits disclosing or reporting a fellow police officer's wrongdoings, even serious criminal activities, as identified by the Knapp and Mollen Commissions (Ivkovic, 2003; Klockars et al., 2004; Knapp, 1973; Mollen, 1994; Skolnick, 2002). According to Skolnick, "the code both impedes the internal investigation of corrupt officers and encourages the junior officers to be a part of a lawless world threatening them with the label of 'rat or cheese eater' (p. 12). The same code and brotherhood can develop into a subculture that results in tolerance of a colleague's violation of criminal law and creates a criminal police subculture. This unwritten code is so widespread that it has been found to be a characteristic of policing across continents. The code is discussed by Punch (1985, 2003) in the study of scandals in New York, London, and Amsterdam, and by Fitzgerald (1989) in Queensland. The concern of this study is police officers' peer reporting decisions. The study seeks to understand whether police officers' peer reporting decisions are determined by the features of the organization, by individual characteristics, usually referred to as the "bad apple theory" (Ivkovic, 2003; Trevino & Youngblood, 1990), or by the features of the features of the ethical issue itself.

Theoretical Framework

Ethical decision making is defined as the process through which individuals make judgments and decisions considering the factors involved in the situation as to the goodness or badness, or wrongness or rightness of a moral issue (Carlson, Kacmar, & Wadsworth, 2002; Kardasz, 2005; Rest, 1984, 1986). Beginning from the mid-1980s, the subject of individual ethical decision making has received increasing attention (Ford & Richardson, 1994). This is partly due to the increased focus on descriptive ethics which is concerned with describing and explaining the morality of human behavior. Most studies in this area have taken two general approaches to elaborate the morality of human behavior; either cognitive developmental psychology or the social learning perspective (Rest, 1984, 1986; Pollock, 2007). Several authors view developments in descriptive ethics as a natural consequence of greater awareness among the general public, interest groups, and politicians because of the unethical events in business, government, and military institutions which occurred in the 1970s and 1980s (Carlson et al., 2002; Detert, Trevino, & Sweitzer, 2008). Likewise, Sherman (1982) argues that police unethical events, such as police corruption, are part of "the larger problem of official corruption in American society" and "a demonstration of the incidence of unethical actions at every level of government" (p. vii).

Therefore, in an effort to better predict and explain the individual ethical decision making process and the factors related to this process, a variety of ethical decision making theoretical models have been proposed by academicians and researchers. Among them, Rest's (1984, 1986), "four-component model," Trevino's (1986) "person-situation interactionist model," and Jones' (1991) "issue-contingent model" have received the most attention. These models form the theoretical foundations of the current study. These models are presented in brief, but they are discussed in greater detail later in Chapter II.

In 1984, Rest introduced the "four-component model" to explain the individual level ethical decision making process. The model includes four components: moral recognition, moral judgment, moral intent, and moral behavior. More specifically, Rest argues that to behave morally in a particular situation, a person must first recognize the existence of a moral issue in the situation; second, the person must make a moral judgment to determine what course of action is right or wrong or just in the situation; third, the person must establish an intention to take the moral line of action; and, finally, the person must follow through the moral intent he/she developed and engage in moral behavior.

In 1986, Trevino wrote about the importance of the characteristics of the workplace on individual ethical decision making. Trevino proposed a general theoretical model that explains individual ethical/unethical decision making within organizational settings, "a person-situation interactionist model." The model transforms the individual approach to an interactionist approach incorporating individual factors with organizational and contextual factors.

The third theoretical model used in the current study is "an issue-contingent model" presented by Jones in 1991. Jones criticized the existing models of ethical decision making that failed to consider the characteristics of ethical issues and argued that the moral issue itself might have profound influences on individual ethical decision making. The most important concept of Jones' model is "moral intensity" which is used to capture the nature of the moral issue in question. Moral intensity is defined as "the extent of an issue-related moral imperative in a situation" (Jones, 1991, p. 372). According to Jones, the intensity of a moral issue is captured by six characteristics: magnitude of consequences, social consensus, probability of effect, temporal immediacy, proximity, and concentration of effect.

Most of the empirical studies that attempt to predict and explain individual ethical decision making thus far have been conducted in the area of business ethics, medical ethics, and environmental ethics, while the systematic study of ethics in criminal justice professions has been a neglected issue (Caldero & Crank, 2004; Gold, 2005; Sherman, 1982). To the best knowledge of the researcher, upon a thorough and careful search through major electronic databases in the social sciences using keywords drawn from the theoretical models of interest, no empirical study has tested these ethical decision making theoretical models collectively in the policing literature. Therefore, the current study uses these major theoretical models in the area of ethical decision making and investigate police officers' ethical decision making with regard to peer reporting.

Research Questions

Because the ethical decision making models presented above suggest that many factors can influence an individual's ethical decision making within organizations, it is not possible to investigate all of the suggested factors in one study. Therefore, the study investigates the influences of selected individual demographic, dispositional, organizational, and issue-related factors on police officers' ethical decision making with regard to peer reporting.

The demographic factors are the police officer's age, gender, race, length of service, marital status, and supervisory status. Dispositional factors include police officers' attitudes toward ethics and cynicism. Situational factors include the magnitude of consequences and social consensus. Organizational variables include referent others and reinforcement contingencies. There are five specific research questions that this study aims to answer.

1) What influences do individual demographics have on police officers' ethical decision making with regard to peer reporting?

2) What influences do individual dispositional factors have on police officers' ethical decision making with regard to peer reporting?

3) What influences do organizational factors on police officers' ethical decision making with regard to peer reporting?

4) What influences do issue-related factors have on police officers' ethical decision making with regard to peer reporting?

5) Which one of these individual, organizational, and issue-related factors has the strongest influence on police officers' ethical decision making with regard to peer reporting?

The Organization of This Book

In this introductory chapter, the purpose and the problem under the investigation, peer reporting, have been identified. The theoretical frameworks that form the foundations of this study and the specific questions that this study investigates have been also presented.

Introduction

The main purpose of Chapter II is to develop a working model for the purpose of this study, which is to investigate police officers' peer reporting decisions. Therefore, Chapter II provides a thorough literature review, which begins with the definitions of the relevant ethical concepts and the philosophical foundations of study of ethics. Then, a review of the ethical decision making models that form the foundations of the current study are presented. Also, the individual, organizational, and issue-related factors proposed to influence an individual's ethical decision making in the literature are presented. Finally, the theoretical model developed for the current study is displayed in Figure 4.

Chapter III presents a thorough literature review of the main concern of this study, police officers' peer reporting intentions. The concepts of moral intent and peer reporting are defined and reviewed. Then, empirical studies related to the factors proposed to influence police officers' ethical decision making with regard to peer reporting are examined along with a background discussion of the individual, organizational, and issue-related factors.

Chapter IV discusses the overall methodology used in this study. First, it introduces the research questions and hypotheses. Because this study uses secondary analysis, the data and methodology used in the original study, the sample, the research design, and the data collection techniques are explained and discussed. Strengths and weaknesses of the data collection methodology and survey instrument also are identified in this section. The measurement of the independent and dependent variables also is presented. Chapter IV concludes with a data analysis plan that describes the statistical techniques that will be used to test the hypotheses.

Chapter V explores the data used in the current study. A number of different statistical analyses were computed to assess the accuracy of coding and imputing the data, missing values, and the influences of the extreme values. Reliability and validity of scales also are discussed. Then, bivariate relationships between the study variables are considered. Finally, OLS regression analysis is conducted to test the hypotheses, and the results of the statistical analysis are presented.

In the final chapter of this book, the findings of the study with regard to each hypothesis and the strengths and limitations of the study are discussed. The book concludes with some implications for police organizations, police administrators, and future research.

CHAPTER 2

Theories of Ethical Decision Making

For centuries, philosophers and academicians have discussed and examined ethics and the semantics of ethical concepts. Despite this, Ford and Richardson (1994) contend that many studies do not provide clear definitions of ethical concepts. Ethics is a branch of philosophy; and ethical concepts are intangible, complex, and confusing. According to Souryal (2007), these characteristics make the study of ethics challenging; but these same characteristics also give beauty to the study of ethics. It is important to understand certain concepts and terms related to this study to make these concepts as clear as possible.

Everyone makes decisions and judgments involving ethics in daily day life. However, not all decisions and judgments are the concern of ethics. Pollock (2007) and Jones (1991) similarly argue that only human decisions and actions when freely performed and involving an ethical issue are questions of ethics.

An *ethical issue* is defined as a particular situation where the *moral agent's* decision and action in response to the situation has the potential to affect (harm or benefit) the well-being of other parties involved in the situation (Jones, 1991; Trevino & Nelson, 2004). The presence of an ethical issue is necessary for a decision to be considered ethical or unethical. A *moral agent* is a person who is involved in an ethical issue and who makes an ethical decision (Jones & Ryan, 1997).

Ethical decision making, from the process perspective, is defined as the process through which individuals make judgments and decisions as to the goodness or badness, or wrongness or rightness of a moral issue (Carlson et al., 2002; Kardasz, 2005; Rest, 1984, 1986). An *ethical decision* is defined as "both legally and morally acceptable to the larger community" whereas "an unethical decision is either illegal or morally unacceptable to the larger community" (Jones, 1991, p. 367). From the pro-social perspective, an ethical decision is a pro-social behavior engaged in with moral motives, such as to protect and promote the well-being of all parties involved in the situation (Staub, 1978).

In this study, *police unethical behavior* refers to a broad set of illegal or unethical actions, from accepting free gifts and meals, and using excessive force, to stealing something (i.e., a watch or a wallet) from a burglary scene. Such a broad definition of police unethical behavior is adopted here because it allows for inclusion of various illegal, unethical, and illegitimate police practices and behaviors. This also places respondents in situations with varying levels of moral intensity and allows the researcher to measure variations in their peer reporting intentions, which was a limitation observed in previous studies (i.e., Felkenes 1984).

Ethics and morality: The concepts of *ethics* and *morality*, and *ethical* and *moral* are frequently used interchangeably to judge whether human conduct or a decision is right or wrong, or good or bad (Braswell, 2005; Jones, 1991; Pollock, 2007; Souryal, 2007). Consistent with much of ethical decision making research, the terms ethics and morality are used interchangeably. As such, the "goodness" or the "badness" of a behavior may be expressed by describing it as either moral/ethical or immoral/unethical. These terms have similar root meanings as well. For example, e*thics* is derived from the Greek word "ethos" and relates to a person's character and behaviors, and *morality is* derived from the Latin word "mores" or "moralitas" that refers to character and proper behavior (Pollock, 2007; Braswell & Miller, 1992). However, while they do overlap, ethics and morality also differ from each other (Braswell & Miller, 1992; Souryal, 2007).

Today, the term "ethics" is used by many to define what is good and bad, and/or right and wrong within a profession or an organizational setting (Braswell & Miller, 1992; Pollock, 2007). Ethics is a branch of philosophy, and it is defined as the science or study of the morality of human behavior (Albanese, 2008; Banks, 2004). It is an "...inquiry into the nature and grounds of morality where the term morality is taken to mean judgments, standards, and rules of conduct"

(Taylor, 1975, p. 1). Ethics seeks to examine the moral philosophy of human conduct, the goodness and badness, or rightness and wrongness of human behavior, drawing on complex philosophies, such as teleology and deontology (Pollock, 2007; Souryal, 2007). The scope of the study of ethics is broad, and it includes a wide range of human behaviors and statements as well as their consequences (Souryal, 2007).

Morality, on the other hand, refers to collections of moral principles and norms and "the practice of these principles on a regular basis, culminating in a moral life" (Souryal, 2007, p. 18), or, as Pollock (2007) describes it, "the total person" (p. 10). Morality refers to good conduct and acceptable or permissible behavior whereas immorality refers to bad conduct or unacceptable conduct (Albanese, 2008; Braswell & Miller, 1992). Morality is shaped and learned through personal experiences with those around us in society involving family, school, religion, and work as these properties impose certain norms, values, and principles to be followed (Braswell & Miller, 1992; Braswell, 2005; Souryal, 2007). All humans make moral decisions and choices in everyday life and regulate behavior in reference to certain moral principles, which constitute the morality of a person (Braswell & Miller, 1992; Pollock, 2007).

A *value* may be defined as "an enduring belief that a specific mode of conduct or end-state of existence is personally or socially preferable to (its) opposite" (Rokeach, 1973, p. 5). More specifically, values are judgments of worth of something about which individuals care and attach importance. They can include behaviors and attitudes (i.e., honesty, loyalty, and friendship), social desires, and properties (i.e., autonomy, power, and family) (Albanese, 2008; Banks, 2004; Pollock, 2007). Individuals can organize their value preferences and choices, which make up a *value system*. A *value system* is "a rank ordering of values along a continuum of importance (Rokeach, Miller, & Synder, 1971, p. 158), or "an enduring organization of beliefs concerning preferable modes of conduct or end-state of existence" (Rokeach, 1973, p. 5).

A review of ethics literature also shows that ethics has several branches or subject areas, such as *meta-ethics, normative ethics*, and *descriptive ethics* (Pollock, 2007). *Meta-ethics* investigates the nature and meaning of ethical statements, concepts, and principles that normative theories suggest. It is concerned with the logic, reasoning, and language used in the definition, justification, and verification of these moral statements, concepts, and judgment (Pollock, 2007; Souryal, 2007). For example, meta-ethics seeks to answer questions, such as what the terms good, bad, wrong, and right mean.

Normative ethics is the larger and more substantive field that is concerned with more practical issues. That is, normative ethics is prescriptive in that it involves defining moral standards and principles to follow and determines sanctions that govern the conduct (Souryal, 2007). Normative ethics sets out ethical standards and establishes moral duties and determines "what people ought to do" in an ethically involved situation (Banks, 2004; Pollock, 2007, p. 10). Arguably, normative ethics teaches us our duty to do the right thing.

Souryal (2007) argued that meta-ethics and normative ethics are interrelated or interconnected to one another in such a way that meta-ethics investigates and evaluates the quality and validity of moral properties suggested by normative ethical theories and contributes to normative ethics providing criticisms. Souryal views this connection as similar to the relationship between courts: A court of primary jurisdiction represents normative ethics, and an appellate court represents meta-ethics. Each contributes to the other.

The study of normative ethics can be divided into two main categories: *teleology*, which is concerned with the consequences of the action, and *deontology*, which is concerned with the intrinsic value of the action itself (Souryal, 2007; Pollock, 2007). These theories are briefly reviewed below.

Teleological Theory

The root of "teleology" comes from the Greek terms "teleios," which means "consequence" and "logos," which means study (Gold, 2005; Souryal, 2007). Teleological theory, also known as end-based or consequentialist theory deals with the consequences of an action and determines the moral worth of an action judging its consequences. As such, regardless of the qualities of the action engaged in, the action is judged to be morally good if it produces good consequences; and an action is judged to be morally bad if it produces bad consequences (Pollock, 2007; Souryal, 2007). Clearly, teleologists are not concerned with motives or intentions that affect the action; they focus on outcomes of the action and determine the moral status of the action based on these outcomes.

Utilitarianism is one of the most popular teleological theories that defines and determines what is good and good for whom from the perspective of hedonism. Jeremy Bentham (1748-1832) and John Stuart Mill (1806-1873) are the pioneers of utilitarianism, and they set forth the main principles of utilitarian theory. According to the theory, for an action to be morally good, that action ought to produce happiness for the majority (Pollock, 2007; Souryal, 2007). Mill (1979) maintains that "there is in reality nothing desired except happiness" (p. 37). Happiness is the fundamental good that all people desire and it is identified by biological, emotional, and aesthetic pleasure. In contrast, pain and suffering are bad consequences that no one desires (Gold, 2005).

Deontological Theory

Deontology is not concerned with the consequences of an action but with the act itself regardless of what the consequences of the act are. The deontologist believes that there must be something inherent in the act that makes the act moral or immoral, and that is good will or intent (Pollock, 2007; Souryal, 2007; Gold, 2005).

Deontology has its roots in two Greek terms: "deontos," meaning duty, and "logos," meaning study. Therefore, deontology is the study of duty (Pollock, 2007; Souryal, 2007). Immanuel Kant (1724-1803) is one of the most famous deontology theorists (Gold, 2005; Souryal, 2007), who focused on the concept of duty and the good will or intent, the two most important concepts in the study of morality that utilitarianism virtually fails to consider. That is to say, individuals must take certain actions to perform their duties; actions even that can result in bad consequences. As such, a police officer has the duty to issue a ticket to a motorist driving over the speed limit though the action gives pain or displeasure to the driver (Gold, 2005).

Another important concept is good will. Kant (1964) maintains "it is impossible to conceive of anything in the world, or even out of it, which can be taken as good without qualification, except good will" (p. 61). For Kant, the fundamental good without any qualification is good will, and that determines the moral status of an action. No matter what the consequences of an action are, that action is morally good if accompanied by good will, but morally wrong if committed with an evil intention or selfish purposes (Gold, 2005; Souryal, 2007).

Most of the earliest theoretical models in the study of ethics were based on the normative/prescriptive ethical theories, which aimed to improve the ethical practices of individuals within organizations (Fritzsche & Becker, 1984; Cavanagh, Moberg, & Velasquez, 1981). For example, Fritzsche and Becker (1984) surveyed a random sample of 593 managers to investigate the relationship between normative ethical theories (i.e., utilitarian and deontological) and marketing managers' behavior. The managers' responses to a series of scenarios involving various business ethical problems (i.e., coercion and conflict of interest) were sorted according to the ethical theory they represented. The findings showed that the majority of the managers adopted a utilitarian approach, considering the consequences of the acts portrayed in the vignettes, in their responses. In this study, rather than the actual behavior of the respondents, their intentions were measured. Given the difficulty measuring the actual behavior, it is common to measure intention in the study of ethics since intentions are viewed as the best predictors of subsequent behavior (Ajzen & Fishbein, 1977), and moral intent may result in moral behavior (Ferrell & Gresham, 1985; Trevino, 1986).

Although normative ethics is important in the study of ethics, this mode of inquiry has received little empirical attention (Ford & Richardson, 1994; Loe, Ferrell & Mansfield, 2000; Reidenbach & Robin, 1988). As discussed previously, normative ethical theories are not intended to explain individual decision making processes for situations with an ethical content. Rather, normative ethical theories are prescriptive and proscriptive in that they define and determine moral concepts, duties, and moral standards for improving the ethical practices of individuals (Souryal 2007; Pollock, 2007; Trevino, 1986; Loe et al., 2000). Additionally, Reidenbach and Robin (1988) contend that the pluralistic nature of normative ethics poses another problem to the study of ethics. That is, the existing normative ethical theories present conflicting definitions, rules, and standards in ethical terms, and provide multiple individual and ideological approaches. In brief, what is ethical for one approach may not be ethical for another.

In addition, some researchers (Ferrell & Gresham, 1985; Hunt & Vitell, 1986) have discussed various normative ethical theories and postulated that moral philosophies influence individuals when making ethical decisions. They have reduced their models to teleology and deontology excluding the other streams of moral philosophy, such as

Theories of Ethical Decision Making 15

ethics of justice, relativism, or virtue. Trevino (1986) further argued that normative theories do not make sense because there is a low probability that individuals will think of normative theories in situations involving ethical issues. As such, from the utilitarian perspective, a decision maker should predict the possible impact of each alternative course of action on all stakeholders and choose the action that maximizes the good of the majority, which is a difficult task.

Descriptive Ethics

The criticisms mentioned above led to advancements in descriptive ethics and the presentation of a number of theoretical models to better explain and predict individual ethical decision making, especially during the 1980s (Loe et al., 2000; O'Fallon & Butterfield, 2005). Descriptive ethics is defined in various ways by researchers, but the definitions presented below imply similar meanings.

Descriptive ethics is concerned with people's decisions and behaviors and seeks to explain and predict why people act the way they do (O'Fallon & Butterfield, 2005), "how people actually make ethical decisions" (Trevino & Nelson, 2004, p. 88), and/or what actually occurs in the organization (Loe et al., 2000). Descriptive ethics is the social scientific study of ethics (Trevino et al., 2006). Researchers seemed more keen to study descriptive ethics rather than normative ethics because descriptive ethics aims to describe what actually occurs in organizations and explains why people behave the way they do. Moreover, as previously discussed, normative ethics is difficult to empirically study whereas descriptive ethics is more suitable for empirical analysis (Loe, Ferrell, & Mansfield, 2000).

Descriptive models, also called positive models, propose to examine the individual ethical decision making process by introducing various factors (i.e., individual and situational) that could influence an individual's ethical decision making (Loe et al., 2000). These models aim to better predict what keeps individuals from making good ethical decisions and to propose solutions to overcome these obstacles or determine what helps individuals to make ethical decisions (Trevino & Nelson, 2004).

These models generally identify and propose a number of key personal characteristics (i.e., gender, education, and cynicism), organizational (i.e., significant others, rewards and punishment, and organizational culture), and situational (i.e., the intensity of moral issue) factors that may influence individual ethical/unethical decision making behavior. The most popular models are: Dubinsky and Loken's (1989) ethical decision making in marketing, Ferrell and Gresham's (1985) contingency framework for marketing ethics, Hunt and Vitell's (1986) general theory of marketing ethics, Jones' (1991) issue contingent model, Rest's (1984, 1986) theory of individual ethical decision making, and Trevino's (1986) person situation interactionist model. In this study, Jones' (1991), Rest's (1986), and Trevino's (1986) ethical decision making models are utilized because these models offer a general theory of ethical decision making that can be used to examine individual ethical decision making in police organizations. The other three models (Dubinsky & Loken, 1989, Ferrell & Gresham, 1985; Hunt & Vitell, 1986) are excluded because they are offered to explain marketing and business ethics specifically.

Ethical Decision Making

The interest in the social scientific study of ethics has increased since the second half of the twentieth century (Trevino & Weaver, 2003). In general, this is viewed as a natural consequence of greater awareness among the public due to highly visible scandals that occurred in public and business organizations (Detert et al., 2008; Trevino, 1986; Trevino et al., 2006). Likewise, Sherman (1978) argues that police unethical events especially in the form of police corruption revealed by commissions are part of "the larger problem of official corruption in American society" and "a demonstration of the incidence of unethical actions at every level of government" (p. vii).

In this context, while ethically relevant police activities and issues can be traced to the foundations of early police departments in America (Barker, 2006; Barker & Carter, 1994; Goldstein, 1975), police ethics as a topic of interest became a concern among Criminal Justice (CJ) researchers and scholars in the mid-1980s (Kleinig, 1996). These ethically relevant activities in organizations led to the development of theoretical frameworks and empirical research about the influences of various factors on ethical and unethical behavior in organizations (Trevino & Weaver, 2003).

Some researchers have adapted psychological, social psychological, and/or sociological contextual perspectives and have developed various theoretical models aimed at identifying the relevant factors that influence ethical and unethical behavior in organizations (i.e., Ferrell & Gresham, 1985; Jones, 1991; Rest, 1984; Trevino, 1986). Others have utilized these theoretical models and investigated how these factors describe and explain individual ethical decision making and behavior in organizations (i.e., Haines, Street, & Haines, 2007; Harrington, 1997; Mayo & Marks, 1990; Reidenbach & Robin, 1988, 1990; Robin, Reidenbach, & Forrest, 1996; Paolillo & Vitell, 2002). For example, nursing, education, counseling, accounting, dentistry, and sports have interested researchers who try to understand how ethical and unethical decision making and behavior occur in organizations.

Police ethics, with respect to social scientific scrutiny, has been a neglected issue (Caldero & Crank, 2004; Gold, 2005; Sherman, 1982). The existing literature shows that the bulk of the work and writing on this topic is theoretical and normative, rooted in the humanities, such as philosophy, or anecdotal (Albanese, 2008; Banks, 2004; Braswell, McCarthy, and McCarthy, 2005; Braswell & Miller, 1992; Goldstein, 1975; Kleinig, 2008; Sherman, 1978; Souryal, 2007). However, understanding what influences police officers' ethical decision making and behavior can provide critical insights and help develop interventions intended to improve the ethical decisions of police officers.

As far as the empirical literature concerning police ethics is concerned, police corruption has received the greatest attention from researchers. Since the 1970s, police corruption has become a popular topic due to widely publicized incidents of police corruption investigated and identified by commissions in a number of cities, including New York City (the Knapp Commission, 1973, and the Mollen Commission, 1994), Philadelphia (the Philadelphia Police Task Force, 1987), and Los Angeles (the Christopher Commission, 1996) (Barker, 1977, 1978; Barker & Roeback, 1974; Ivkovic, 2003; Klockars et al., 2000).

On the other hand, the existence of the problem of police corruption is not just peculiar to the police in America, but it occurs throughout the world. Sherman (1985) and Ivkovic (2003) similarly point out that no police department from Los Angeles to Tokyo and from New York to Rio de Janeiro is completely immune from corruption, and corruption always is possible where there are police. Although the problem has been occurring less frequently when compared to the past, it still persists (Raymond & Terrance, 2004).

According to Caldero and Crank (2004), police corruption has received the greatest attention because police corruption is tangible and relatively easy to study. However, there are few empirical works on police corruption. One of the reasons for this paucity is the unwillingness of police officers to admit and reveal police corruption (Ivkovic, 2003). Ivkovic argues that police officers have no incentives or motives to report their own or to report another police officer's corrupt activities because they are the members of the police subculture that supports the "code of silence" (p. 603). In these published studies, researchers have taken two different types of approaches in their inquiry of police corruption, either individual or organizational (Klockars et al., 2004).

Absent from this growing interest in the study of ethically relevant police practices is a consideration of individual factors along with issue-related and organizational/contextual factors that might influence ethical decision making and behavior in police organizations. These three dimensions of ethical decision making are important as individual ethical decision making and behavior are situated within psychological, social psychological, and sociological contexts in organizations (Trevino & Weaver, 2003). However, no study that directly tested a model with the explicit intention of investigating police officers' ethical decision making has been found in the policing literature.

Therefore, the current study focuses on individual/psychological, social psychological, and the sociological context within which ethical issues arise and police officers make ethical decisions. Also, this study intends to be the first study to directly test a model of ethical decision making with regard to peer reporting built upon the existing ethical decision making theoretical models found in the literature. The ethical decision making frameworks that inform this study include Rest's (1984) individual psychological model, the "four-component model," and from the organizational social psychology perspective, Trevino's (1986) "person situation interactionist model," and Jones' (1991) "issue-contingent model" of ethical decision making.

Cognitive Moral Development Theory:

It would be appropriate to start the discussion by presenting a brief review of Kohlberg's (1969) theory of cognitive moral development as the theory has made important contributions to advancements in descriptive ethics and has been the theoretical basis for many subsequent ethical decision making theories (Rest, 1986; Rest & Narvaez, 1994; Trevino, 1986).

Research in morality and moral judgment to predict ethical/unethical behavior started with the work of Jean Piaget (1932), who studied children's moral development and found that moral reasoning involves a series of developmental stages. However, it was not until the work of Lawrence Kohlberg in 1950s and 1960s, who followed the Piagetian tradition, that this topic gained prominence. Kohlberg challenged the predominant approach in morality by claiming that individuals are capable of determining what is right and wrong (Rest & Narvaez, 1994).

Kohlberg (1958) devised the Moral Judgment Interview (MJI), a qualitative questionnaire instrument that included several hypothetical scenarios with ethical content. He interviewed people from different age groups longitudinally. Kohlberg believed that moral reasoning brings about moral choices and behavior. Thus, he focused on individual moral reasoning processes and sought to explore differences in a respondent's reasoning and problem solving skills through responses to scenario based questions. Having conducted a series of studies that examined moral development from different age groups ranging from 8-to-48, Kohlberg (1969) introduced a cognitive moral development theory, also called stage theory of moral reasoning that describes the structure of human moral reasoning, choices, and behavior.

Briefly, Kohlberg's theory postulates that moral judgment is a conscious process, and individuals advance in their moral reasoning through an invariant and irreversible six stages. These stages are combined into three levels and are used to describe and identify an individual's level of moral judgment, which is assumed to be positively related to an individual's moral decisions and behavior. For example, Level 1 is the pre-conventional level at which individuals are not able to recognize social rules and expectations. Individuals at this level are egocentric, and try to avoid punishment and seek personal gratification and satisfaction. Most children under the age of nine are at the pre-conventional level of reasoning. Level II is the conventional level at which individuals are able to recognize the necessity of social rules and laws and have internalized them. Individuals at this level are ethnocentric and willing to receive external expectations and try to do good deeds. Most adolescents and adults are at the conventional level of reasoning. Level III is the post-conventional level. Individuals at this level are world-centric and able to recognize broader and universal moral standards and principles. Fewer people, usually adults above the age of twenty, can reach the post-conventional level of moral thinking.

In 1979, Rest developed a multiple choice test, called the Defining Issues Test (DIT), which was later modified and updated (DIT2) in 1999, by Rest, Narvaez, Thoma, and Bebeau. The DIT used some of Kohlberg's (1969) scenarios and was designed to measure the moral development construct. Since the time it was developed, the DIT has been used extensively in over 40 countries, and it has been shown to be a valid and reliable test for moral reasoning development (Rest & Narvaez, 1994; Trevino et al., 2006). For example, Rest (1986) combined 10-year longitudinal data and reported that older and more educated people have a higher stage of moral reasoning than younger and less educated people.

However, education is a stronger predictor of moral reasoning development than merely chronological age. People who stopped their formal education showed little advancement in moral reasoning compared to people who continued their formal education. Gender was not found to be associated with moral reasoning. What makes education the strongest predictor of moral development? Rest (1986) argued that "the people who develop in moral judgment are those who love to learn, who seek new challenges, who enjoy intellectually stimulating environments, who are reflective...and who take responsibility for themselves and their environs" (p. 57).

On the other hand, Kohlberg's theory of cognitive moral development has been criticized for several reasons, such as for focusing largely on justice based theories of morality (Gilligan, 1982; Trevino et al., 2006) and being "too rationalistic and individualistic" (Rest & Narvaez, 1994, p. 7). Gilligan (1982), the most famous opponent of Kohlberg's theory, contended that the theory does not explain the moral development of women, who are care oriented (i.e., protecting others from harm and considering the well-being of others) and follow a distinct path of moral development different than men, who also are justice oriented.

The theory also was discredited for being too rigid in the stage advancement and not particularly useful in explaining context specific and real life human behavior. For example, Krebs, Denton, and Wark (1997) found that respondents' behavioral responses to real-life situations do not correspond to their level of moral reasoning determined through responses to Kohlbergian based philosophical scenarios. Mesmer-Magnus and Viswesvaran (2005) in their meta-analyses of studies investigated intention to report peers' unethical behavior and the actual reporting of unethical behavior. They observed that moral judgment is moderately related to intention to report peers' unethical behavior (r = 0.45) whereas it is not related to the actual reporting of unethical behavior (r = - 0.08). This suggests that individuals may not operate in real-life situations at the level of development identified by the theory.

The Four-Component Model:
Drawing heavily on developmental theories related to moral reasoning (e.g., Kohlberg, 1969), Rest introduced a four component model of the "process involved in the production of moral behavior" for the first time in 1984 (p. 19), and a modified version of the model later in 1986 and 1994. Rest argued that individual ethical decision making and behavior are a product of complex and multifaceted psychological processes, rather than a unitary, single process. The model includes four distinct cognitive components: 1) moral awareness (also referred to as ethical or moral sensitivity, or moral recognition); (2) moral judgment (Kohlberg, 1969); (3) moral intent or motivation; and (4) moral behavior. Clearly, Rest's model perceives ethical decision making to be a rational process and behavior to be a product of interactions among moral sensitivity, moral judgment, and moral intent components rather than solely a product of moral judgment as suggested by Kohlberg's theory of moral development.

Rest (1986) argued that to make moral decisions and behave morally a person should be able to recognize the ethical aspects of the situation, and be aware of the available courses of action and their possible effects on all parties involved including oneself. Moral sensitivity is assumed to trigger or start the ethical decision making process which could probably result in a moral decision and/or behavior.

The second component draws upon cognitive moral development theory (Kohlberg, 1969) and proposes that the person engages in a conscious moral reasoning process searching, weighing the facts, and inferring what course of action is right or wrong among the possible courses of actions available in the situation.

Moral intent or motivation is the third component. The person distinguishes and prioritizes certain moral values and goals relative to other values and goals (i.e., individual and organizational) and establishes an intention in favor of the morally right course of action favorable to others. The final process is called moral character; and it assumes that the person should have sufficient skills, like courage, perseverance, and ego strength, to be able to follow through on the moral intent he/she has developed. Then he/she engages in moral behavior. Figure 1 shows Rest's (1986) model.

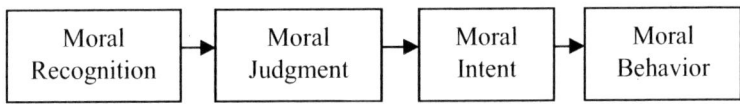

Figure 1. The four-component model of individual ethical decision making proposed by Rest (1984).

For the model, Rest (1986) pointed out several issues. First, the components of the model should not be taken as virtuous traits that make up the ideal moral person, but rather they are cognitive processes used to make ethical decisions. Second, each component has distinct functions to perform, and success in one component does not guarantee success in another. Strengths and weaknesses in any of these processes can result in failure in ethical decision making. For example, a person who does well in identifying the ideal moral option (Component 2) may not always act accordingly (Component 4).

Last and more importantly, one could have the impression that Rest's model proposes a causal relationship among the components in that each component is postulated to causally influence the other component. Rather, Rest (1986) noted that the model does not posit a linear relationship or temporal order among the components as depicted by the model, such that a person first recognizes the moral issue, followed, in turn, by moral judgment, moral intent, and moral behavior. In fact, Rest argued that although these components might interact and influence each other, research suggests that interactions among the components are generally complicated. Weighing the facts and defining what is morally right in a situation (Component 2) may influence the person interpreting the issue (Component 1). Finally, the "four component model" is designed as an analytical tool and a theoretical framework to guide research in this topic rather than to suggest that ethical decision making occurs as a result of a sequential interaction among the four components as the model would appear to offer (Rest, 1986).

Similarly, Trevino and Weaver (2003) argued that a causal relationship among these components, like the one exemplified above, is not certain, but rather "much human behavior takes scripted form in that it is largely automatic, embedded in the routines of life, or triggered by particular contextual clues, and thus devoid of conscious deliberation (component 2)" (p. 161). In their review of studies that examined behavioral ethics in organizations, Trevino et al. (2006) concluded that conscious moral reasoning is neither always sufficient nor a necessary condition for moral behavior, but a high degree of automaticity rather than conscious moral reasoning might produce morally exemplary behavior.

Support for this argument comes from studies conducted by Singhapakdi, Salyachivin, Virakul, and Veerayangkur (2000), and Robin et al. (1996) who similarly found that moral awareness or sensitivity has a positive and substantial influence on ethical intention. Haines et al. (2007) also supported these results; they observed that the inclusion of moral sensitivity substantially increased the amount of explained variation in moral intention in all scenarios; in fact, moral sensitivity in four of the five scenarios was a stronger predictor of moral intent than moral judgment.

Although the "four component model" is an individual level ethical decision making model, Jones (1991) argues that it can be used to investigate individual ethical decision making within any organizational setting. As a matter of fact, numerous studies based on Rest's four components of ethical decision making have been conducted in various disciplines, such as education, nursing, accounting, and sports (Rest & Narvaez, 1994), but there is little research that has utilized the model in the police ethics literature. Therefore, it is reasonable to utilize Rest's model of ethical decision making in police organizations and investigate police officers' ethical decision making. The focus of this study is the moral intent component of Rest's individual ethical decision making model. The selected factors proposed to influence the moral intent component are investigated to predict police officers' peer reporting intentions.

It is important to note that most studies about factors on moral action have investigated the moral intent component as an outcome variable instead of the moral action component (O'Fallon & Butterfield, 2005). This is normal because ethically charged behavior is difficult to observe and measure as methods used to investigate the ethicality of a behavior could affect the behavior (Trevino, 1986). Another reason is the fact that intention is the closest variable to moral behavior (Ferrell & Gresham, 1985; Rest, 1986; Trevino, 1986), and the strongest determinant of moral behavior (Ajzen & Fishbein, 1980).

The literature has shown that an individual's behaviors often have been found to be consistent with his/her intentions (Victor, Trevino, & Shapiro, 1993). In a more recent review of studies about ethical decision making, O'Fallon and Butterfield (2005) and several other researchers report that there is little research that has investigated Rest's "four component model" in its completeness, and only a few studies have investigated the causal relationship among two or more components (Barnett, 2001; Carlson et al., 2002; Haines et al., 2007; May & Pauli, 2002; Robin et al., 1996; Trevino & Weaver, 2003). Most ethical decision making research in organizations has sought to predict one of each of the three stages investigating the factors thought to influence these components. Consistent with the literature, this study investigates police officers' ethical decision making intentions of peer reporting.

Rest's framework has some limitations. Namely, although Rest (1986) maintains that morality is an extremely complex phenomenon, "rooted in the social conditions and the human psyche" (p. 1), he focuses on only the latter, the human mind. He identifies the complex cognitive processes through which an individual makes an ethical decision, but fails to explain other social forces that could influence the decision making process. This is because Rest largely draws on human rationality and consciousness and assumes that individuals are able to make moral decisions through reasoning. Rest's singular focus on the human psyche is somewhat expected since James Rest is a psychologist, and a former student of Lawrence Kohlberg.

It also can be argued that the model neglects to consider the failures and the limitations of human rationality in making decisions, which means that humans have "bounded rationality" (Simon, 1957). Moral decision making is constrained by many external and internal factors. As such, individual decision making may be constrained by time and by incorrect or incomplete information about the facts of the situation about which a decision is to be made (Cornish & Clarke, 1987), as well as by the features of human nature, such as selfishness, struggle for power, concentration on momentary consequences, and disregard of long term consequences (Simon, 1957).

From this, one must not necessarily conclude that ethical decision making is constrained only by human cognitive boundaries. Rather, when it comes to individual ethical decision making in an organizational setting, ethical decision making is further constrained by organizational/contextual and issue-related factors, especially when personal values and goals are not concordant with the organizational ones. Therefore, if one wants to study ethical decision making in organizational settings, Rest's ethical decision making model alone is insufficient and it should be reinforced or strengthened with the consideration of other ethical decision making models to better explain and predict ethical decisions by members of organization.

In their critical review of studies that tested the relationship between moral judgment and moral behavior (i.e., honesty, cheating, delinquency, and peer reporting), Blasi (1980) and Rest (1986) consistently reported a statistically significant relationship but a medium effect size of about .3 between the two variables. This suggested that moral judgment does not fully account for moral behavior and that the relationship is "less direct and more complex" (Blasi, 1980, p. 9). Furthermore, there are extraneous or confounding variables; "variables not accounted for nor measured in the present studies are also determinants" (Rest, 1986, p. 135).

In an effort to better understand and predict individual ethical decision making within organizations, various interactionist ethical decision making models have been proposed by researchers (Hunt & Vitell, 1986; Dubinsky & Loken, 1989; Ferrell & Gresham, 1985; Jones, 1991; Trevino, 1986). All of these models generally incorporate various individual factors with organizational/contextual and issue contingent factors aimed at better predicting and explaining ethical decision making in organizations. The discussion below examines the interactionist theoretical model proposed by Trevino. This is followed by Jones' (issue-contingent model).

A Person-Situation Interactionist Model:
Trevino (1986) was interested in explaining individual ethical/unethical decision making and behavior within organizational settings. She expanded the existing perspective of moral psychology on ethical decision making and offered a general theoretical framework that emphasized the important influence of workplace on an individual's ethical/unethical decision making within organizational settings. According to Jones (1991), Trevino proposed a general ethical decision making model, "a person-situation interactionist model" that explicitly draws on the concept of moral judgment presented by Kohlberg (1969) and implicitly on Rest's (1984) "four-component model." Trevino incorporated individual cognitive and dispositional factors with organizational and contextual factors, transforming Rest's individual approach to an interactionist approach, in an attempt to better predict and explain individual ethical decision making within organizational settings.

The model includes the individual factors of ego strength, field dependence, and locus of control. Organizational/contextual job factors include reinforcement contingencies, and referent others; elements of organizational culture consisted of normative structure, obedience to authority, and responsibility for consequences. Characteristics of the work factors include role taking and resolution of moral conflict. Based on Trevino's interactionist model of ethical decision making, this study investigates the influences of reinforcement contingencies and referent others on police officers' peer reporting decisions. Figure 2 shows Trevino's (1986) model.

```
┌─────────────────────────────┐
│ Individual Moderators: Ego  │
│ Strength, Field Dependence, │
│ Locus of Control            │
└─────────────────────────────┘
                │
                ▼
┌──────────┐   ┌──────────────────┐   ┌──────────────────┐
│ Ethical  │──▶│ Cognitions: Stage │──▶│ Ethical/Unethical│
│ Dilemma  │   │ of Moral          │   │ Behavior         │
│          │   │ Development       │   │                  │
└──────────┘   └──────────────────┘   └──────────────────┘
                         ▲
                         │
┌─────────────────────────────────────────┐
│ Situational Moderators: Reinforcement   │
│ and other pressures, Organizational     │
│ Culture (normative structure, referent  │
│ others, obedience to authority, and     │
│ responsibility for consequences), and   │
│ Work Characteristics                    │
└─────────────────────────────────────────┘
```

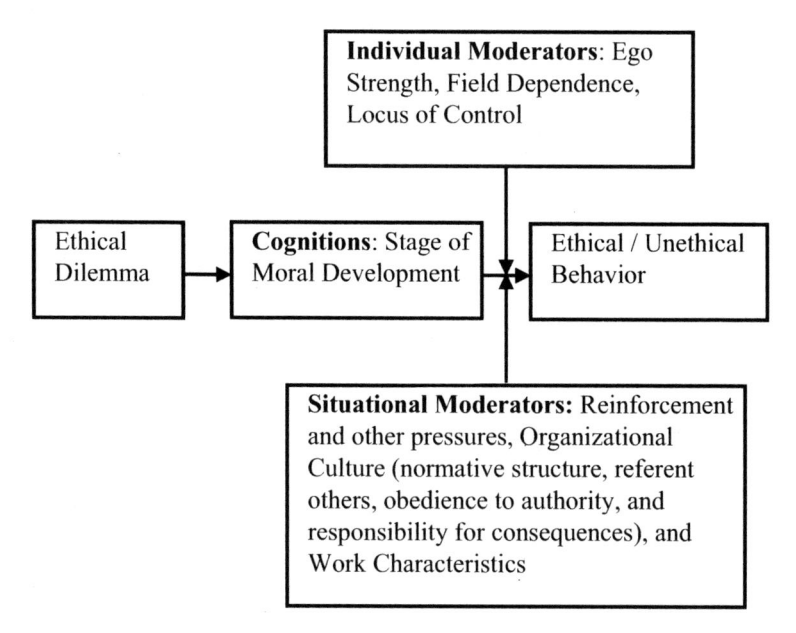

Figure 2. The person-situation interactionist model shows the factors that can influence an individual's ethical decision making in organizations (Trevino, 1986).

An Issue-Contingent Model:
Until the early 1990s, the study of ethical decision making had been preoccupied with individual and organizational perspectives or some combination of them. Those from the individual perspective assumed unethical organizational behavior due to a few "bad apples" attributing the problem to individual characteristics. Those from the organizational perspective assumed the problem was due to "bad barrels" attributing the problem to organizational factors (Ivkovic, 2003; Trevino & Youngblood, 1990). Conversely, interactionists, such as Hunt and Vitell (1986) and Trevino (1986) argued that neither the individual perspective nor the organizational perspective was sufficient to explain unethical organizational behavior and proposed interactionist theoretical models that incorporated individual factors with organizational factors.

Jones (1991) criticized the previous models for failing to consider the important role of the ethical issue itself in the generation of ethical/unethical decision making and behavior and proposed his "issue-contingency" model. It was not until Jones introduced his model that researchers examined the ethical issue itself and realized that it might influence an individual's ethical decision making. Particularly, Jones notes "if the models making up this synthesized model of ethical decision making and behavior are taken at face value, the moral decision-making and behavior process of individuals in organizations is identical for all moral issues" (p. 371). This quote suggest that Jones' focus is not the moral agent or the moral environment but the moral issue itself, and that ethical decision making is dependent on characteristics of the moral issues.

Jones (1991) introduced the concept of "moral intensity" to define and identify the characteristics of a moral issue. Moral intensity is defined as "the extent of issue-related moral imperative in a situation" (p. 372) and it is used to capture the nature of the moral issue in question. According to Jones, the moral intensity of an ethical issue includes six characteristics: magnitude of consequences, social consensus, probability of effect, temporal immediacy, proximity, and concentration of effect.

Magnitude of consequence is related to the extent of the consequences of a moral issue and proposes that the moral intensity of an issue will be high if the consequences are greater, rather than fewer. Social consensus refers to the degree of social agreement concerning the morality of an issue and proposes that the greater the social consensus, the greater the moral intensity of the issue. Probability of effect suggests that an issue will be more intense if the consequences of the action in question are highly likely to occur, rather than less likely to occur. Temporal immediacy proposes that an issue will be more intense if the consequences will occur in a shorter time, rather than a longer time. Proximity of effect suggests that an issue will be more intense if the consequences influence the decision maker. Concentration of effect proposes that an issue will be more intense when fewer people are affected by the consequences of a given magnitude rather than the same consequences being broadly distributed.

Jones (1991) also provided definitions of ethical and unethical decisions that he contended were missing in the previous models (i.e., Trevino, 1986, Hunt & Vitell, 1986). An ethical decision is defined as "both legal and morally acceptable to the larger community" whereas "an unethical decision is either illegal or morally unacceptable to the larger community" (p. 367). Figure 3 shows the Jones' model.

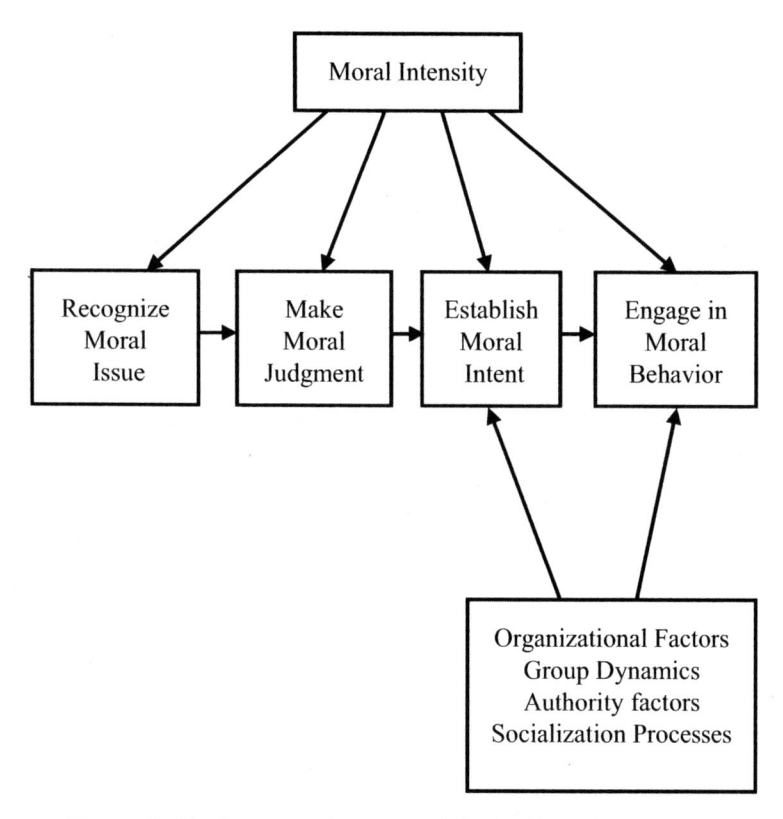

```
                    ┌──────────────────┐
                    │  Moral Intensity │
                    └──────────────────┘
                     ↙    ↓    ↓    ↘
┌──────────┐   ┌──────────┐   ┌──────────┐   ┌──────────┐
│ Recognize│→  │   Make   │→  │ Establish│→  │ Engage in│
│  Moral   │   │  Moral   │   │  Moral   │   │  Moral   │
│  Issue   │   │ Judgment │   │  Intent  │   │ Behavior │
└──────────┘   └──────────┘   └──────────┘   └──────────┘
                                  ↑              ↑
                    ┌──────────────────────────────┐
                    │   Organizational Factors     │
                    │      Group Dynamics          │
                    │     Authority factors        │
                    │   Socialization Processes    │
                    └──────────────────────────────┘
```

Figure 3. The issue-contingent model of ethical decision making proposed by Jones (1991).

In summary, Jones' (1991) model synthesizes past ethical decision making models and incorporates individual and contextual organizational factors with a new set of variables called "moral intensity" to better predict individual ethical decision making within organizational settings. Trevino's (1986) and Jones' models incorporate Rest's (1986) "four component model" with other individual (i.e., ego strength and locus of control), organizational (i.e., referent others and reinforcement contingencies), and issue-related factors (i.e., magnitude of consequences and social consensus) and seek to better predict and explain individual ethical decision making within organizational settings. The two models modify and transform Rest's four component model from an individual approach to a situationist and interactionist approach.

These three ethical decision making models together were used as the foundations of the peer reporting model that the current study tested to describe and explain police officers' peer reporting intentions. These models along with a review of the empirical literature on ethical decision making guided the selection of variables and the development of the peer reporting model for the current study.

Antecedents of Ethical Decision Making

The existing ethical decision making models have suggested a number of factors influencing individual ethical decision making from different perspectives. These model perspectives have employed a moral reasoning process, which focuses on the moral agent investigating the underlying cognitive processes of morality (e.g., Kohlberg, 1969; Rest, 1984, 1986), a moral environment perspective, which focuses on factors external to the moral agent identifying and delineating the organizational and contextual determinants of ethical decision making (e.g., Trevino, 1986), or a situational perspective, which focuses on the characteristics of the moral issue that influence ethical decisions (Jones, 1991). Therefore, factors thought to influence ethical decision making can be categorized into three main categories: individual, organizational, and situational.

Among these three categories, individual factors have been the most frequently examined factors (Ford & Richardson, 1994; Loe et al., 2000; O'Fallon & Butterfield, 2005). This is not surprising since individual demographics, such as age and gender, frequently are employed as control mechanisms in social science studies to remove their confounding effects (Punch, 2005).

Demographic Factors:

A review of the existing literature concerning ethical decision making illustrates that the individual variables of age, gender, work experience, and education (type and years) consistently have been found to be insignificant and unrelated to ethical decision making. The majority of the studies that have investigated the influences of these variables on ethical decision making have found that these variables either have no significant influence or that the findings were inconclusive due to mixed results (Loe et al., 2000; O'Fallon & Butterfield; 2005).

For example, in their review of ethical decision making studies Ford and Richardson (1994), Loe et al. (2000), and O'Fallon and Butterfield (2005) collectively reported on 74 studies that investigated the relationship between gender and ethical decision making. Among these studies, gender was found to be unrelated to ethical decision making in 39 studies (e.g., Brady & Wheeler, 1996; Dubinsky & Levy, 1985). Only a few studies found that gender was significantly related to individuals' ethical decision making where women made more ethical decisions than men (e.g., Borkowski & Ugras, 1998; Ferrell & Skinner, 1988; Ross & Robertson, 2003).

As for the relationship between age and ethical decision making, the findings have been generally mixed and inconclusive. That is, of 38 studies reviewed, 14 found little or no age differences (e.g., Izraeli, 1988; Ross & Robertson, 2003). In 16 studies, age was positively related to ethical decision making (e.g., Ruegger & King, 1992; Sankaran & Bui, 2003); but age was negatively related in 8 studies (e.g., Hunt & Jennings, 1997).

The existing literature has shown that the link between ethical decision making and education (type and years) and tenure (work experience) also is inconclusive. Of 14 studies that investigated the influence of type of education or major on ethical decision making, 10 found little or no significant differences (e.g., Dubinsky & Ingram, 1984), and 3 studies produced mixed results. One study found than non-business majors made better ethical decisions than business majors (Sankaran & Bui, 2003).

In the ethics literature, a great majority of studies reported that the higher the education level, the higher the ethical judgments, when an individual's ethical judgment is measured through the DIT score. These findings also were reported in King and Mayhew (2002), who reviewed 172 studies conducted on the moral judgment component of Rest's framework. They indicated that with the exception of two studies, the remaining 170 found that moral judgment is an outcome of higher education. As previously mentioned, the positive influence of education on moral judgment development also was observed in Rest's (1986) review.

As for the work experience factor, in 11 studies, work experience was found to have no significant or only a marginal influence on ethical decision making (e.g., Wu, 2003). Only a few studies found a positive link between work experience and ethical decision making suggesting that more experienced employees made better ethical decisions than less experienced employees (Dawson, 1992; Weeks, Moore, McKinney & Longenecker, 1999).

In summary, a great deal of attention has been focused on the influences of individual demographics in the ethical decision making literature. On the other hand, the bulk of studies have generally shown that age, gender, education, and work experience variables do not appear to be significantly related to individuals' ethical decision making. Higher education has been the most predictive variable of the second component of Rest's (1984) model, moral judgment. Few studies have found individual differences in ethical decision making, and, in general, more experienced employees, women, and older people are more likely to make ethical decisions than other employees.

Dispositional Factors:
Various individual difference variables have been associated with ethical decision making. For example, Machiavellianism, locus of control, and moral philosophy variables have been shown to be related to ethical decision making. Machiavellianism, in general, is negatively related to ethical decision making (Jones & Kavanagh, 1996; Singhapakdi & Vitell, 1990). Individuals with an internal locus of control tend to take responsibility for their actions and see the connections between their behaviors and its consequences. By contrast, individuals with external locus of control tend to attribute consequences of their actions to other factors, such as fate and luck (Trevino et al., 2006; Trevino & Youngblood, 1990). Research has shown that external locus of control is negatively related to ethical decision making (Jones & Kavanagh, 1996), while internal locus of control is positively related (Cherry & Fraederich, 2002). Ethical philosophies (deontological, teleological, relativism and idealism) consistently have been found to

be related to ethical decision making. For example, deontological considerations are found to be more influential in ethical decision making than teleological considerations (DeConinck & Lewis, 1997), and relativism is positively related to ethical decision making while idealism is negatively related (Barnett et al., 1996; Sparks & Hunt, 1998; Yetmar & Eastman, 2000).

Cynicism is another dispositional factor posited and investigated as a potential predictor of the ethical decision making process, which is reviewed in detail later in this chapter. For example, Anderson and Bateman (1997) and Detert et al. (2008) investigated the influence of cynicism on ethical decision making among administrative and professional employees and undergraduate students respectively. Both studies found that cynicism is significantly and negatively related to ethical decision making. Individuals make better ethical decisions as their levels of cynicism decrease.

The current study approaches the study of ethical decision making with regard to peer reporting intentions from a somewhat different perspective by testing a model that includes two individual dispositional factors, cynicism and attitudes toward the code of ethics. Specifically, the current study investigates the relationship between police officers' levels of cynicism, attitudes toward code of ethics, and their behavioral intentions with regard to peer reporting.

Organizational Factors:
Various organizational factors have been proposed to influence individual ethical decision making within organizational settings. These factors include the existence of codes of ethics, rewards and sanctions, and ethical climate (Ferrell & Gresham, 1985; Trevino, 1986); and research findings suggest that they appear to predict individual ethical decision making in organizations. The existence and enforcement of a code of ethics consistently have been found to be positively related to individuals' ethical decision making in organizations (e.g., Ferrell & Skinner, 1988; Singhapakdi & Vitell, 1990; Weaver & Trevino, 1999).

Rewards and sanctions also have an impact on ethical decision making. That is, rewarding unethical behavior increases unethical behavior and intentions to engage in unethical behavior (Shapeero, Koh, & Killough, 2003; Trevino & Youngblood, 1990) while perceived punishment or risk of punishment for unethical behavior decreases intentions to engage in unethical behavior (Cherry & Fraedrich, 2002;

Glass & Wood, 1996). However, Trevino and Weaver (2003) contend that rewarding ethical behavior is the strongest predictor of ethical decision making. An organizational ethical climate factor proposed by Victor and Cullen (1988) has been found to be positively related to ethical decision making in organizations (Loe et al., 2000; O'Fallon & Butterfield, 2005). Ethical climate is defined "as a shared perception among organization members regarding the criteria (e.g., egoism, benevolence, and principle) and focus (e.g., individual, group, and society) of reasoning within an organization" (Trevino et al., 2006, p. 966). Organizations with strong ethical climates are more likely to have employees who make good ethical decisions and to have less serious ethical problems than organizations that have a weak ethical climate (Bartels, Harrick, Martell, & Strickland, 1998; Trevino, Butterfield, & McCabe, 1998).

Referent others, based on the premises of social learning theory (Akers, 1985; Sutherland, 1947), is another organizational factor proposed to influence individual ethical decision making within organizational settings in some ethical decision making theories (e.g., Ferrell & Gresham, 1985; Jones, 1991; Trevino, 1986). The theory suggests that unethical behavior like ethical behavior is learned through interactions with others within intimate referent groups. In their review, Loe et al. (2000) examined 11 studies regarding peer influences on ethical decision making and reported that peer group influence has been found to have a strong influence on ethical decision making.

Based upon this knowledge and previous research regarding organizational factors, this study proposes to test a model of reporting peer unethical behavior that includes two organizational factors. Specifically, the current study investigates the influences of peers and reinforcement contingencies on police officers' intentions to report peer unethical behavior.

Situational Factors:
Moral intensity theory proposed by Jones (1991) identifies and defines the characteristics of the moral issue and assumes that individual ethical decision making is contingent upon the perceived significance or seriousness of these factors existing in the nature of the moral issue. As previously discussed, the issue-related factors include magnitude of consequences, social consensus, and probability of effect, temporal immediacy, proximity, and concentration of effect.

Theories of Ethical Decision Making 35

A number of studies have investigated the link between moral intensity dimensions and ethical decisions. For example, in their review of 32 studies conducted on moral intensity, or some component of moral intensity, and ethical decision making, O'Fallon and Butterfield (2005) reported fairly consistent findings and strong influences. That is, with the exception of one study, the remaining 31 studies found a link between moral intensity components and ethical decision making. Among the components of moral intensity construct, magnitude of consequences and social consensus dimensions consistently have been found to have the strongest influence on ethical decision making processes when compared to other moral intensity dimensions. For example, Barnett (2001) and Barnett and Valentine (2004) found that magnitude of consequence and social consensus were significant predictors of ethical decision making while proximity and temporal immediacy had no significant influence.

Based on this discussion and consistent with previous research about this topic, the current study tests a model that predicts police officers' intentions to report peer unethical behavior that includes two components of moral intensity. Specifically, the study investigates the influences of magnitude of consequences and social consensus factors on police officers' intentions to report peer unethical behavior.

The next chapter focuses on moral intent and peer reporting of unethical behavior, which is the primary concern of this study. Figure 4 shows the theoretical model of this study.

Independent Variables

Demographic Variables: Age, Gender, Race, Years of Service, Marital Status, and Rank.

Dispositional Variables: Cynicism and Attitudes toward Ethics.

Organizational Variables: Peer Association and Reinforcement.

Issue-related Variables: Seriousness of the Ethical Issue and Social Consensus.

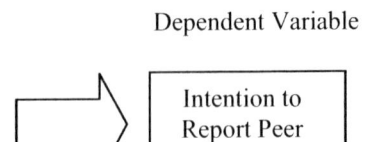

Dependent Variable

Intention to Report Peer Unethical

Figure 4. The theoretical model of the current study.

CHAPTER 3

Factors Associated With Peer Reporting

The primary purpose of the current study is to investigate police officers' ethical decision making intentions. Particularly, this study focuses on a special case of ethical decision making, that of peer reporting of unethical behavior. Peer reporting is a special type of ethical decision making behavior, and it has been one of the positive outcome behaviors investigated in the ethical decision making literature (Trevino et al., 2006). However, there is very little research concerning peer reporting of unethical behavior in the policing literature. Therefore, the current study focuses on police officers' decisions to report peer unethical behavior.

As mentioned previously, the majority of studies on ethical decision making have focused on and investigated moral intent as a proxy to moral behavior. This is due to difficulties in observing and measuring ethically charged behavior accurately. In doing this, researchers used the Theory of Reasoned Action (TRA) proposed by Fishbein and Ajzen (1975). Their theory predicts a link between intent and behavior in that "the best predictor of a person's behavior is intention to perform the behavior" (Fishbein & Ajzen 1975, p. 381) and posits that the stronger the intention, the more likely that the behavior will occur.

Other reasons that researchers are unwilling to investigate actual behavior may be associated with difficulties in locating actual peer reporters and in investigating the actual peer reporting behavior. In fact, actual peer reporters probably would be unwilling to provide information about their actual peer reporting behavior as the information could harm their rights to privacy (e.g., anonymity or confidentiality). In addition, the information the peer reporters provide might imperil the organization's efforts for controlling the problem or preclude an ongoing investigation of unethical behavior. For example, Rothwell and Baldwin (2007) attempted to compare a random sample of 547 police officers and civilian employees in their intentions to blow the whistle on unethical behavior and their frequency in blowing the whistle on unethical behavior. However, analyses with regard to frequency of blowing the whistle were omitted due to insufficient information. Therefore, moral intent in many ethical decision making frameworks is identified as a proxy to moral behavior and as a principle concept in understanding and predicting a specific behavior of interest (Dubinsky & Loken, 1989; Hunt & Vitell, 1986; Jones, 1991; Rest, 1984).

Based on the theory of reasoned action and the above mentioned ethical considerations in the investigation of actual behavior, researchers have investigated the influences of various individual, organizational, and issue-related factors on an individual's intentions as predictors of specific ethical behavior. In addition, the link between a person's intention and the person's actual behavior has been supported in that an individual's behaviors often have been found to be consistent with his/her intentions (Bass, Barnett, & Brown, 1998; Beck & Ajzen, 1991; Ferrell & Gresham, 1985). For example, Victor et al., (1993) in their field survey study, investigated respondents' intentions to report theft and their theft reporting behavior in a fast-food restaurant. They found that the respondents' behavioral intentions were indeed significantly associated with their actual reporting behavior.

Green (1989) in a panel study tested deterrence theory - perceived certainty and severity of legal punishment- on individuals' intentions and actual behavior for the offense of driving while under the influence of alcohol and reported a very high correlation (r = .85) between intentions and actual behavior. Based upon this knowledge and consistent with the previous research about this topic, this study investigates police officers' peer reporting intentions of unethical behavior as key to understanding police officers' actual behavior when they face similar issues.

Moral Intent Defined:

Moral intent is identified and defined in several ethical decision making models in a similar fashion. As such, Dubinsky and Loken (1989) define moral intent as 'the individual's subjective probability that he or she will engage in behavior" (p. 85). In Hunt and Vitell (1986), the intention construct is conceptualized as "the likelihood that any particular alternative will be chosen" (p. 9). In Rest's "four component model" of ethical decision making, moral intent is identified as a precursor to moral behavior and defined as the "degree of commitment to taking the moral course of action, valuing moral values over other values, and taking personal responsibility for moral outcomes" (Rest et al., 1999, p. 101). At this stage a person distinguishes and prioritizes moral values above other values (i.e., personal) and establishes an intention to take the morally right course of action (Rest, 1986). Similarly, Jones (1991) argues that at the moral intent stage, a decision maker establishes intent as to what to do weighing moral factors against other factors before engaging in a particular behavior.

Peer Reporting

Goldstein (1975) and Sherman (1978) contend that unethical behaviors of police officers have tremendous consequences on the quality of police services and the well-being of society, especially with respect to public confidence in the police. For example, it is estimated that the latest police corruption scandals in the Los Angeles Police Department can ultimately cost the city $200 million (Davidson, 2000). There may be intangible costs that can result from police unethical behaviors as well.

Peer reporting of unethical behavior is suggested as a potential supplementary control mechanism to cope with employees' unethical behavior within organizations when other control mechanisms are insufficient (Trevino & Victor, 1992). This is based on the assumption that peers are more likely to be knowledgeable of colleagues' unethical behaviors (Trevino & Victor, 1992). Likewise, Miceli and Near (1985) argue that "whistle-blowers can conceivably help organizations to correct unsafe products or working conditions or to curb fraudulent or wasteful practices and, thereby, to avoid substantial adverse consequences, such as harm to clients, customers, or employees and resulting loss of sales..., and negative publicity" (p. 526).

When officers report peer unethical behavior in police organizations, it can be a potential tool for controlling and preventing police unethical behaviors. For example, police administrators may benefit from peer reporting and might encourage police officers' reporting behavior of unethical behavior. It is important to understand the factors influencing peer reporting behavior. This can help guide police administrators to determine whether it is individual or organizational contextual factors in which peer reporting behavior occurs and proceed accordingly.

Peer Reporting Defined:
Peer reporting is characterized as a special type of whistle-blowing (Barnett et al., 1996; Trevino & Victor, 1992) and has been one of the positive outcome behaviors investigated in the ethical decision making literature (Trevino et al., 2006). The term whistle-blowing is analogous to "an official on a playing field, such as a football referee, who can blow the whistle to stop action" (Miceli & Near, 1992, p. 14). Whistle-blowing is conceptualized as "the disclosure by organization members (former or current) of illegal, immoral, or illegitimate practices under the control of their employers, to persons or organizations that may be able to affect action" (Miceli & Near, 1985, p. 4). This definition of whistle-blowing has been widely accepted and used by researchers who are interested in this topic (Barnett et al., 1996; Mesmer-Magnus & Viswesvaran, 2005; Trevino & Victor, 1992; Victor et al., 1993).

According to the definition, whistle-blowing has three critical dimensions: whistle-blower, the person to blow the whistle (former or current); recipient of the report of wrongdoing who is able to take action and solve the problem; and, finally, action (s) that is not just in violation of the laws but also immoral or illegitimate to organization practices. Additionally, whistle-blowing can occur in two forms; either reporting superiors' unethical or questionable actions to higher supervisors or governmental authorities or reporting of a peer's unethical behaviors to superiors who can cope with the problem in an organization (Trevino & Victor, 1992). Studies about reporting superiors' unethical behaviors rather than reporting a peer's unethical behavior have appeared in the literature (Barnett et al., 1996; Miceli & Near, 1992). By contrast, this study is focused on peer reporting of a peer's unethical behavior.

Based upon its ability to identify the dimensions of whistle-blowing behavior and its acceptance in the whistle-blowing literature, a slightly modified version of the Miceli and Near (1985) definition is used in this study. For the purposes of this study, peer reporting is defined as the disclosure by a police officer of illegal, immoral, or illegitimate practices of another police officer in the organization.

Independently, the peer reporting process also is conceptualized from two different perspectives. First, it is a decision making process involving ethical considerations, such as perceived seriousness of the unethical behavior suggested by Graham (1986). This makes the link between Jones' (1991) moral intensity theory and peer reporting behavior clearer. Therefore, this study uses Jones' issue-contingency model as a theoretical foundation of the proposed model to predict police officers' peer reporting decisions.

Second, peer reporting is viewed as a pro-social behavior. Pro-social behavior is a behavior that occurs in organizations with moral motives, such as to protect and promote the well-being of all parties involved in the situation (Dozier & Miceli, 1985; Graham, 1986; Miceli & Near, 1992; Staub, 1978). From this perspective, whistle-blowing is an ethical act if it involves moral motives to protect others from any harm, including the organization.

Miceli and Near (1988) suggest that although there is no existing theory of whistle-blowing, predictors of pro-social behavior also may be used to predict whistle-blowing behavior in organizations. Consistently, research generated from these whistle-blowing perspectives has identified and investigated a variety of individual, organizational, and situational correlates of whistle-blowing intentions and behaviors similar to the ethical decision making theoretical models discussed previously. In the section below the empirical findings regarding the influences of selected factors on peer reporting intentions are reviewed, and a hypothesis for each factor is presented.

Demographic Factors

The demographic factors that are associated with peer reporting or whistle-blowing include age, gender, tenure, marital status, and supervisory status (Miceli & Near, 1992). Similar to the empirical results presented previously in the review of the ethical decision making literature, studies that have investigated the link between these demographics and whistle-blowing have produced inconsistent results.

Age:
Miceli and Near (1992) argue that "it is difficult to assume whether younger members will be more or less likely to blow the whistle than older members" (p. 116). Still, they predict that younger members are less likely to blow the whistle based on the assumptions that younger employees would be less knowledgeable about wrongful behaviors, feel less responsible for reporting unethical behaviors, and have high career aspirations that might inhibit them from blowing the whistle. Some studies found older organization members to be more likely to blow the whistle on unethical activities (Brewer & Selden, 1995; Dworkin & Baucus, 1998; Miceli & Near, 1988) while other studies found younger organization members to be more likely to blow the whistle on unethical activities in organizations (Keenan & Sims, 1995; Parmerlee, Near, & Jensen, 1982).

Gender:
With regard to the link between gender and whistle-blowing, men are perceived as more likely to blow the whistle than are women (Miceli & Near, 1992). For example, several researchers found that men are more likely to blow the whistle than women (Graham, 1989; Keenan & Sims, 1995; Miceli, Dozier, & Near, 1991; Miceli & Near, 1984; Miceli, Near, & Schewenk, 1991; Sims & Keenan, 1998). However, in two studies, gender was unrelated to whistle-blowing (Dworkin & Baucus, 1998; Fritzsche, 1988).

Work Experience:
Work experience or tenure also is posited to be positively related to whistle-blowing. This is based on the assumption that more experienced employees would be more familiar with the whistle-blowing procedures, closer to retirement, implying less to lose, and/or more willing to correct organizational problems due to their greater organizational commitment (Miceli & Near, 1992). However, the link between tenure and whistle-blowing is inconclusive due to the mixed results reported in previous research.

For example, tenure was not found to be related to whistle-blowing in three studies (Rothwell, 2003; Sims & Keenan, 1998; Singer,

Mitchell, & Turner, 1998), while longer work experience was associated with whistle-blowing in two other studies (King & Hermodson, 2000; Miceli & Near, 1988). In Dworkin and Baucus (1998), individuals with shorter work experience were found to more likely to blow the whistle on unethical activities than individuals with longer work experience. Of these studies, the Rothwell (2003) study was the only one that had a sample composed of 300 randomly selected police officers. The findings revealed that police officers' years of experiences were not significantly related to police officers' peer reporting intentions (Rothwell, 2003).

Supervisory Status and Marital Status:
Other individual demographics thought to influence a person's whistle-blowing behavior include supervisory status in an organization and marital status (Miceli & Near, 1992). More specifically, marriage is assumed to provide some tangible (financial) and intangible (personal) support and to increase the possibility of whistle-blowing intentions. People who are married are more likely to engage in whistle-blowing because they will have less expected costs of their whistle-blowing actions than people who are unmarried (Miceli & Near, 1992).

Supervisory status also is posited to be positively related to whistle-blowing. That is, individuals who hold a supervisory position in an organization are more likely to engage in whistle-blowing for a member's wrongdoing than non-supervisors (Jos, Tompkins, Hays, 1989; Miceli & Near, 1984, 1992). On the other hand, Dworkin and Baucus' (1998) quantitative and qualitative analysis of 33 cases of whistleblowers who were wrongfully fired for reporting wrongdoing found no relationship between supervisory status and whistle-blowing on wrongdoing.

A study by Rothschild and Miethe (1999) surveyed 761 employees nationwide from a number of organizations and professions, such as a manufacturing company and university personnel. They also reanalyzed data from the U.S. Merit System Protection Board (1993) on more than 13,000 federal employees. They found that supervisory position and marital status variables do not explain differences in whistle-blowing among the members of organizations investigated.

In summary, although the empirical results with regard to individual differences are inconsistent, it appears that employees who are male, older, married, supervisors and have more work experience are more likely to blow the whistle than others. The following hypotheses for individual demographics are offered for investigation.

H1: Older police officers are more likely to have peer reporting intentions than younger police officers.

H2: Male officers are more likely to have peer reporting intentions than female officers.

H3: Police officers who have more work experience are more likely to have peer reporting intentions than police officers who have less work experience.

H4: Police officers who are married are more likely to have peer reporting intentions than police officers who are not married.

H5: The higher the supervisory status, the higher the peer reporting intentions.

H6: There is no race difference among police officers in their peer reporting intentions.

Dispositional Factors

An individual's predisposition also may be related to the person's ethical decision making and behavior (Miceli & Near, 1992). A predisposition is defined as "an inclination or bias from one's past" (Morris, Rehbein, Hosselni, & Armacost, 1995, p. 125). Theoretical models of ethical decision making (e.g., Dubinsky & Loken, 1989; Ferrell & Gresham, 1985; Trevino, 1986) recognize characteristics of the individual as predictors of ethical decision making and behavior. Similarly, Miceli and Near (1992) hold that "individual difference variables probably should help to predict who will blow the whistle after observing wrongdoing" (p. 49).

<u>Cynicism:</u>
This section of the literature review deals with cynicism, an individual dispositional factor proposed to influence human behavior (Anderson & Bateman, 1997; Detert et al., 2008), and one that must be considered when predicting a person's decisions about an ethically problematic situation (Baumhart, 1961; Trevino, 1986). This section discusses the origin of the concept of cynicism in the literature of policing and briefly reviews and critiques the empirical literature about this topic.

In the policing literature, cynicism was first examined and described by Arthur Niederhoffer (1967), a former New York City police officer. Since then, interest in this topic has increased among social scientists and police scholars (Hickman, 2005; Johnson, 2007; Monahan, 1977; Regoli, Crank, & Rivera, 1990; Regoli & Poole, 1979). In his seminal work "Behind the Shield," Niederhoffer (1967) set forth the theory of police cynicism and conducted a study to explain why some police officers become cynical. Niederhoffer argued that there are three major sources of police cynicism: the police professionalization movement, the police socialization process, and anomie. Niederhoffer used the concept of anomie borrowed from Durkheim (1893, 1897), and proposed the theoretical framework for police cynicism derived from Merton's (1938) work on anomie theory.

Durkheim (1893, 1897) wrote about the process of transition from a mechanical society to an organic society which grew from rapid technological and economical advancements and urbanization. Human societies transformed from simple primitive units to more complex and civilized large cities. To Durkheim, the transition from mechanical to organic society created social crises and the feelings of nothingness, frustration, and alienation among people. There were no clear moral standards, rules, and laws to comply with in society. Durkheim viewed this state of normlessness as anomie.

Merton (1938) borrowed Durkheim's anomie term and from a social structural perspective used it to explain high crime rates in the U.S. Briefly, anomie occurs in society when culturally prescribed norms and values are weakened or disregarded among people in society. Anomie also may result from the discrepant or unequal distribution of legitimate opportunities among all layers of society. Some people who experienced blocked opportunities, more likely the poor and minorities, felt frustrated and strained. This, in turn, led them to utilize illegitimate means to attain the culturally prescribed goal, called the "American Dream." However, not everyone who experiences these anomic conditions and who feels high levels of strain attempts to use illegitimate means to attain the goals; rather, people can develop different responses to their strain. Merton describes five adaptations to strain: conformity, innovation, ritualism, retreatism, and rebellion.

Niederhoffer (1967) used the concept of anomie to better explain police cynicism. Niederhoffer viewed the professionalization movements that occurred in American policing during the 1930s as the transition from traditional policing to modern policing or as the transition from occupation to profession like the transition Durkheim explained from a mechanical society to an organic society. During this transition, besides technological advancements and innovations, such as two way radios and patrol cars employed to improve the quality of police services and an individual officer's performance, higher education, high standards of admission, longer periods of police training, and a code of ethics for police were adopted by police organizations. As a result, police departments became more complex, and police work became highly specific in its division of labor analogous to Durkheim's organic society.

The transition from occupation to profession brought about an "unintended consequence" (Bennett & Schimitt, 2002, p. 495), anomie, within police institutions and subsequent cynicism as an escape from the strain caused by anomie (Hickman, Piquero, & Piquero, 2004). Niederhoffer contended that cynicism is endemic to police and used as a method of adaptation by both newer police officers and "old-school" police officers to mediate and reduce their levels of strain.

For example, the old-school police officers viewed these new policing standards and mores as a threat to their traditional police mores and order. The professional model of policing puts more emphasis on the protection of civil rights and the legally authorized collection of evidence. The old-school officers thought that the ideology of "tough cop" was waning and tried to protect their hegemony within police organizations (Niederhoffer, 1967, p. 4). They rejected the professionalism standards and the accompanying means to carry out police work.

Also, old-school officers became envious and hostile toward newer police officers, in part, because they assumed that newer police officers would be more successful in promotional exams because they had more education and were more likely to be selected from middle-class backgrounds. These conditions fostered non-professional police officers' cynicism toward the professionalism movement, newer officers, the department, and police work as an adaptation to the strain that resulted from anomie within police organizations (Niederhoffer, 1967).

The police socialization process and the realities of police work also are proposed to be factors related to the development of police cynicism. It is argued that new generation police officers are more idealistic, tolerant, and like "social scientist police officers" who adopt the police role of public servant (Niederhoffer, 1967, p. 4). These idealistic police officers tend to be eager to carry out their tasks according to the rules they were taught in the academy. They soon recognize that "doing things by the book" is not usually possible (Hickman, 2005, p. 11); and they experience severe conflicting norms and values "between the professional idealistic view of police work and the pragmatic precinct approach" that make them frustrated with police work (Niederhoffer, 1967, p. 52).

As Sherman (1982) portrays it, after a new recruit leaves the academy, he often will be told on the first day by his senior colleague to "forget everything that had been taught and I will show you how police work is really done" and continues "on this job, your partner is everything. He tells you how to survive on the job... how to walk, how to think... and what to do (p. 13). Faced with the "reality shock" about police work, the idealistic police officer feels perceived loyalty to fellow officers is essential for survival and accepts the old values and norms (Niederhoffer, 1967, p. 48).

Niederhoffer (1967) argued that police officers' "reality shock" continues to grow with their experiences with the public, mass media, and the Criminal Justice system. These factors also could lead to cynicism. That is, police officers always expect respect from the public as the police provide services to the public; but the general public views the police occupation as a low-prestige occupation and police officers tend to be from the lower-class. Young police officers in their early days in police work were sometimes ridiculed; and they were the target of nasty comments from the public. Police also view media as always harsh and unfair toward police as the media demonstrate police wrongdoings and try to uncover police misconduct. According to Niederhoffer, knowledge about the public's perception of police enhances cynicism among the police toward the public.

Police officers also can get frustrated when they exert tremendous effort and risk their lives to apprehend a suspect, and then the suspect receives what they perceive as a lenient sentence. Furthermore, police also are frustrated by court decisions against police practices and tactics used to secure confessions during interrogations and to collect evidence. Young police officers quickly learn that police work is more social work than preventing or reducing crime, the goal they are sworn to carry out. They get frustrated when most of the calls and assignments are for minor issues rather than the "real" police work of catching, arresting, and jailing criminals. They become cynical toward police work and toward their high level managers. Such frustration and strain may lead police to become cynical toward the public, media, and the criminal justice system (Niederhoffer, 1967).

Empirical Findings:
Niederhoffer (1967) developed a cynicism scale to measure police cynicism and administered it to 220 New York City police officers. The instrument consisted of 20 items that were in the form of sentence completion statements with three multiple choice options. He also developed and tested 11 hypotheses to explain police cynicism. Factors proposed to predict cynicism were related to characteristics of a police officer, such as length of service, rank, supervisory status, education level, and type of assignment. To test these hypotheses, Niederhoffer (1967) used 34 newly recruited police cadets (with no experience in policing) and compared them with a total of 144 patrol officers with varying years of police experiences from 2 months to 20 years, and 15 detectives and 27 superior officers.

The most important finding of the study was the length of service; it was the most predictive of police cynicism among patrol officers and had a curvilinear relationship with police cynicism. Cynicism was at its lowest among the Academy recruits, reached the highest level among the police who had 7-to-10 years experience, showed a sharp decline among the police with 11-to-14 years of police experience, and leveled off thereafter to the end of 20 years.

However, the researcher did not control for the type of assignment and rank, and this made the findings spurious. Rank was negatively related to police cynicism, and education was positively related to police cynicism. That is, lower-ranking police officers were more cynical than higher-ranking officers, and less-educated police officers were less cynical than more educated police officers. It was concluded that the socialization process had a significant impact on the development and growth of police cynicism. Niederhoffer (1967) contended that the decline in police cynicism after mid-career was related to the fact that police officers began to realize the realities of police work, and, thus their cynicism waned.

Niederhoffer's work has serious problems regarding the validity of the findings. First, internal validity suffers from other rival hypotheses.

That is, possible extraneous variables, such as type of assignment and officers who left the occupation might have caused the observed decline in cynicism among police officers after 11 years. Second, external validity is subjected to serious biases with regard to sample selection in that some of the respondents were not randomly selected; in fact, they were "persuaded to answer to the best of their ability" (Niederhoffer, 1967, p. 193). Therefore, the findings should be interpreted cautiously as the respondents were not representative of the population from which they were sampled. However, it is important to note that Niederhoffer's study was the first to introduce the concept of police cynicism to the literature of policing and to empirically investigate it.

Since Niederhoffer (1967) introduced cynicism to the policing literature, researchers have attempted to replicate his findings and also to examine the reliability and validity of Niederhoffer's survey instrument. Various methods, such as comparative and cross-sectional research designs, and a variety of individual and organizational factors, such as department size and work relations with others, have been employed to better explain police cynicism.

Regoli (1976a) conducted a survey study in nine different police departments in Washington and Idaho and investigated the reliability and validity of Niederhoffer's original cynicism scale. Regoli changed the response categories of the original instrument to 5-point Likert type response categories and administered it to a sample of 324 police officers composed of mostly patrol officers similar to Niederhoffer's original sample. Analysis for the reliability of the original scale produced an alpha of .66, and principal components analysis showed that Niederhoffer's cynicism construct was a multidimensional construct rather than a one-dimensional construct. The scale virtually contained five relatively distinct areas of policing toward which the police officers could develop cynicism to different extents. Although these five sub-dimensions are categorized differently by others, Regoli identified them as cynicism toward the public, organizational functions, dedication to duty, police and social solidarity, and training and education.

Using the same data from the 1976 study, Lotz and Regoli (1977) investigated the relationship between professionalism and police cynicism which had been defined as two opposite concepts by Niederhoffer but not previously studied. Snizek's (1972) scale contained five dimensions of professionalism, and it was used to measure professionalism. The findings supported Niederhoffer argument in that overall professionalism was found to be inversely related to cynicism. Police officers who were low on professionalism were more likely to score higher in the cynicism survey. They also found the same curvilinear relationship between the length of service and police cynicism, "a gradual increase in cynicism, with a zenith in mid-career, then a gradual tapering off afterwards" (p. 183).

Regoli and Poole (1978) in a cross-sectional study investigated whether police officers develop cynicism to a different extent or whether there are different dimensions of cynicism contrasting two city and county police agencies. Education level, length of police service, and work alienation also were examined from representative samples of two groups of police officers drawn from the two agencies. The findings showed no significant differences observed in overall cynicism scores between city and county police officers. City and county officers were significantly different in their cynicism scores toward the public and toward dedication to duty.

As for the relationship between cynicism and the independent variables of education level, length of police service, and work alienation among city and county officers, city police officers were found to be significantly different than county police officers in their overall cynicism score and its relationship to level of education. Among city police officers, the higher the level of education, the less overall police cynicism. This was not observed among county police officers. City police officers were found to have developed higher levels of cynicism as their length of service increased as opposed to county officers whose overall cynicism scores decreased as the length of service increased. For the relationship between cynicism and work alienation, both city and county officers showed higher levels of cynicism as their work alienation increased.

A study by Regoli, Crank, and Culbertson (1989) employed a different approach and examined the consequences of cynicism on police chiefs' job satisfaction and work relations with other police personnel contrasting large and small departments. A cross-sectional research design was used to collect data from 574 out of 771 Illinois police chiefs through a survey questionnaire. Regoli's (1976a) modification of Niederhoffer's (1967) cynicism scale that yielded two dimensions, cynicism toward the police organization and outsiders, was utilized to measure police chiefs' cynicism. Chiefs from 180 small police departments were contrasted with chiefs from 196 large police departments. The size of police departments were determined based on the number of police officers employed. To obtain a representative sample of departments from small communities, departments with 5 officers or fewer were specified as small and departments of 20 officers or more were categorized as large departments.

Police cynicism in urban departments was found to have a significant and negative impact for 6 out of 8 dimensions of the job satisfaction scale whereas police cynicism in rural departments had a significant and negative impact on only 1 dimension of job satisfaction. Therefore, Regoli et al. (1989) concluded that urban police chiefs who had high levels of cynicism had low job satisfaction. In contrast, among rural police chiefs, cynicism almost had no relationship to job satisfaction. As far as the relationship between cynicism and work relations is concerned, cynicism in urban departments exerted a significant and negative but weak influence on only 3 out of 7 dimensions of the work relations scale whereas cynicism in rural departments exerted a significant and negative influence on 4 dimensions of the work relations scale. Therefore, it was concluded that cynicism had little influence on police chiefs' work relations for both urban and rural departments.

In another study, Regoli et al. (1990) examined the consequences of cynicism on a police officer's job performance. Job performance was specified as work relations with fellow officers, supervisors, and citizens, and arrest records. Police cynicism was specified with four sub-dimensions: cynicism toward (1) police supervisors, (2) rules and regulations, (3) the legal system, and (4) the public and others. Anonymous self-report survey data were collected from a sample which consisted of 110 police officers who had the rank of sergeant or below selected from two agencies in the state of Colorado (no information regarding the sample selection method was provided).

Based on multivariate statistical analyses, the findings indicated that none of the dimensions of police cynicism had any influence on relations with fellow officers while cynicism overall had a significant influence on relations with supervisors with 35% of the explained variation. Police cynicism toward supervisors was the best overall predictor of hostile police citizen encounters. Although police cynicism had no impact on felony arrests, it did affect misdemeanor arrests. This was explained due to the extra-legal factors, such as gender and race of the offender, that increase the likelihood of the use of discretion in handling minor cases like misdemeanors but not in handling felony cases. Therefore, it was concluded that cynicism had an influence on police officers' behaviors. Cynical officers were more likely to have poor work relations, had higher arrest rates, and more hostile encounters with citizens than less cynical officers (Regoli et al., 1990).

Limitations of Cynicism Research:
This review of the police cynicism literature has revealed that most research so far has focused on re-analyzing Niederhoffer's original cynicism scale and predicting the determinants of police cynicism across divergent samples. These studies have found that Niederhoffer's cynicism construct is a multidimensional construct rather than a one-dimensional construct with dimensions ranging from 1 to 6. Although these dimensions are categorized differently, the most widely agreed upon dimensions have been cynicism toward the department and cynicism toward the public. The most predictive factors of police cynicism are the length of police service, department size, education level, and rank (Lotz, & Regoli, 1977; Niederhoffer, 1967; Regoli, 1976b; Regoli et al., 1990; Regoli, & Poole, 1979).

These studies (Lotz, & Regoli, 1977; Niederhoffer, 1967; Regoli, 1976a, 1976b; Regoli, & Poole, 1978) suffered from serious methodological problems. The early studies on police cynicism were correlational studies. A correlational study can show whether the two variables under investigation have an association with one another and demonstrate the magnitude of the association. An association between the two variables is not enough to conclude that there is a causal relationship between the two variables. Thus, these correlational studies are subject to other rival explanations, such as type of assignment, rank, and other district level characteristics like overall crime rates.

By contrast, multivariate statistical techniques could be used to control for the possible influences of multiple factors by investigating these factors simultaneously and attempting to predict which of the variables under investigation is the strongest predictor of the outcome variable (Lewis-Beck, 1980). It also is important to note that the observed curvilinear relationship between the length of service and police cynicism might have been due to patrol officers who left the police force rather than a decline in their cynicism level after mid-career. Thus, a longitudinal study is suggested for future studies to better predict police cynicism.

Studies that utilized multivariate techniques to predict police cynicism also had some limitations. Two studies (Regoli et al., 1989; Regoli et al., 1990) suffered from the internal validity problems of time order and spuriousness. Particularly, police cynicism was utilized as a cause variable to explain outcome variables, such as work relations, police performance, and job satisfaction. However, evidence has shown that cynicism develops and continues after a police officer begins his/her career, along with the proposed effects of cynicism, such as work relations, job satisfaction, and job performance. It is not clearly specified whether cynicism precedes and produces these outcome variables or these variables precede cynicism. Therefore, one criterion of causality, time order, is violated.

In addition, the theoretical models are not clearly identified in order to be able to examine the relationship between police cynicism and its effects and to rule out rival explanations. Rather, the researchers employed multivariate techniques to examine the relationship between the sub-dimensions of cynicism and the sub-dimensions of police performance and job satisfaction. However, they failed to control for the influences of other variables, such as the contextual variables of overall crime rates, population makeup, and neighborhood socio-economic conditions. The proposed relationships in that sense are spurious.

The most recent and comprehensive study by Hickman (2005) examined the impact of police cynicism on police problem behaviors, such as use of force, disciplinary charges, and citizen complaints controlling for the individual variables of age, gender, and race, and contextual district variables like population heterogeneity, district socio-economic status, and residential mobility. Both self-reported data from a randomly selected sample of patrol officers among all Philadelphia patrol officers and official departmental records were utilized for the analyses. The analyses of both official and self-reported data showed that cynicism was a significant predictor of police problem behaviors. Contrary to the most common finding of the previous studies, cynicism in Hickman's study had no significant relationship to length of service.

Cynicism also has been subjected to investigation by researchers in the area of ethical decision making. For example, Detert et al. (2008)

examined the influence of cynicism on ethical decision making among 307 business and education undergraduate students and found that cynicism was significantly and positively related to unethical decision making. Cynical students were more likely to have intentions to engage in the unethical behaviors of stealing, cheating, and lying depicted in the scenarios. A study by Anderson and Bateman (1997) examined the consequences of cynicism in the workplace among 207 administrative and professional employees. Their findings indicated that cynicism significantly increased unethical decisions in the workplace. Cynical employees also were more likely to approve of the company's deceptive advertisement plan (Anderson & Bateman, 1997).

The researcher performed a comprehensive electronic search of the literature to locate studies on police cynicism and ethical decision making. Based on the result of the search, no published study so far has examined the effects of cynicism on police officers' ethical decision making, specifically, on their intention to report a fellow officer's unethical behavior. Based on the review of literature about police cynicism and the discussions above, the current study seeks to determine what effect police cynicism has on police officers' decisions to report a fellow officer's unethical behavior depicted in the scenarios. The hypothesis below is offered for investigation.

H7: The lower the level of cynicism, the more likely police officers will intend to report a peer's unethical behavior.

<u>Attitudes toward Code of Ethics:</u>
A number of studies thus far have investigated the existence and/or enforcement of professional codes of ethics as an organizational factor in the ethical decision making literature. The great majority of these studies consistently found that the existence and/or enforcement of ethics codes is positively related to an individual's ethical decision making and behavior. A summary of these studies and major findings are presented in Table 1.

Table 1

Organizational Factors: Codes of Ethics

Year/Author	Sample	Method	Major Findings
1977 Weaver & Ferrell	280 AMA members	Survey questionnaire	The existence and enforcement of code of ethics improved ethical decision making.
1978 Hegarty & Sims	120 Business graduate students	Experiment	Code of ethics was related to reduced levels of unethical behavior.
1987 Laczniak & Inderrieden	113 MBA students	Experiment	Code of ethics and enforcement of sanctions resulted in more ethical decisions.
1990 Singhapakdi & Vitell	529 AMA members	Survey questionnaire	The existence and enforcement of code of ethics increased seriousness perceptions of ethical problems.
1990 Trevino & Youngblood	94 MBA students	Experiment (in-basket)	Ethics policies increased respondents' ethical awareness and decisions to report unethical behavior in the experimental group.
1992 Weeks & Nantel	309 Salespeople	Survey questionnaire	A well communicated code of ethics was moderately related to job satisfaction and job performance.
1992 Barnett	240 business executives	Survey questionnaire	Formal ethics policies increased ethical awareness and were significantly related to whistle-blowing decisions.

Table 1 Cont.

Table 1

Organizational Factors: Codes of Ethics

Year /Author	Sample	Method	Major Findings
1992 Kaye	50 Australian companies	Survey questionnaire	Codes of ethics increased level of ethical awareness and subsequent whistle-blowing.
1993 Barnett, Cochran, & Taylor	295 Business executives	Survey questionnaire	Formal ethics policies significantly increased reported whistle blowing by employees.
1993 McCabe & Trevino	6096 College students	Questionnaire	Academic dishonesty was significantly higher among students in the institutions with no honor code than among those in the schools with an honor code.
1996 McCabe, Trevino, & Butterfield	318 College graduates	Survey questionnaire	Employees in organizations with codes of ethics reported less unethical behavior.
1999 Weaver & Trevino	420 Finance employees	Survey questionnaire	Values and compliance based ethics programs were both significant and positive predictors of ethical awareness and reporting of unethical behavior.
2001 Trevino & Weaver	1734 Employees	Survey questionnaire	Organization's ethics program follow-through was significant predictor of reporting ethical problems.

Kleinig (1996) argues that because the services provided by the professions are connected to citizens' most important and/or private interests, professionals are guided by a code of ethics. In this context, Weaver and Trevino (1999) state that many American companies have developed formal policy documents such as ethics codes and ethics training programs intended to manage ethics in organizations and guide employees' professional activities and behaviors. To Kleinig (1996), codes of ethics are put forward as public evidence of a "determination, on the part of providers themselves, to serve in ways that are predictable and acceptable" (p. 242). On the other hand, Davis (1998) argues that a professional code of ethics is "a formal statement of a group's ethics and a description of a preexisting practice or a formula creating the practice" (p. 74). Similarly, Barker (2006) argues that a professional code of ethics prescribes guidelines and standards for ethical behavior that apply to all members of a specific occupational group and removes vagueness in individual considerations of what is right or wrong.

According to these definitions, Davis (1998) emphasizes the internal aspect or function of a code of ethics while Kleinig (1996) emphasizes the external aspect of a code of ethics which benefits the public served. To Davis, a professional code of ethics is an agreement between the members of a profession as to what the code prescribes as ethical and unethical. All members of a professional group should adhere to the code thereby optimizing and enhancing the integrity of professional activities. Conversely, Kleinig argues that a code of ethics should aim to "mediate between the providers and users of services" and thereby maintain public trust that certain standards will be reached in the delivery of services (p. 33). Similarly, Delattre (2006) argues that a code of ethics can provide some bases and general guidelines to gain public trust, but "no code can take the place of good character and wisdom" (p. 35).

Police officers are charged with enforcing public laws that specify standards of right and wrong, but public law does not specify or guide how police may act in enforcing the law (Felkenes, 1984). As a result, the police profession through proliferation of a code of ethics tries to provide general ethical guidelines and standards to aid officers in the performance of duties and to improve their ethical decision making and behavior in situations having ethical aspects. Kleinig (1996) views the proliferation of a police code of ethics as a sign of the police desire to gain professional status. This may be true especially in American policing as the early development of a police code of ethics was concurrent with the professionalization movement in American policing launched by August Vollmer in 1930s. However, we know little about the actual influence of these codes of ethics on police officers' professional activities and behaviors.

For example, the "Square Deal" code written by Orlando Winfield Wilson, the Chief of the Wichita (Kansas) Police Department, who was appointed on the recommendation of August Vollmer, is the first code of ethics for American police (Kleinig, 1996). The "Square Deal" code provided the foundation of the International Association of Chiefs of Police's (IACP) code called the Cannons of Police Ethics developed in 1957. The Cannons remained unchanged until 1989. As a result of further changes, two new codes of ethics, the Law Enforcement Code of Ethics and the Police Code of Conduct were created and approved by the IACP in 1991.

The two new codes fulfilled different objectives. The Code of Ethics is a separate code that can be used as an oath of office or pledge made by each law enforcement officer at graduation ceremony (Kleinig, 1996). The Code has been adopted by many police departments both in the United States and internationally (Kleinig, 1996). The Code of Ethics prescribes standards of conduct that each officer:
- perform fundamental law enforcement duties to the best of his/her ability.
- respect the constitutional rights of all people.
- conduct personal affairs so as to reflect on one's Department.
- enforce the law impartially and recognize the public trust implied in the job.
- never employ unnecessary force or violence and accept gratuities.
- never engage in acts of corruption or bribery and condone such acts by other police officers.

The Code of Conduct is somewhat more detailed than the Code of Ethics and contains nine main headings. Each heading represents some ethical standards intended to guide each officer in performing his/her duties and shape his/her ethical decision making, such as primary job responsibilities, limitations of authority, using proper means to gain proper ends, conduct toward the public, gifts and favors, and presentation of evidence. A copy of the Code of Ethics is provided in Appendix A, and a copy of the Code of Conduct appears in Appendix B.

Police Studies:
There is a volume of literature and empirical research concerning ethics especially in the areas of business and marketing, but little empirical research concerning police ethics. For example, Felkenes (1984) investigated the understandings and perceptions of police officers from three agencies about their professional ethics. A total of 103 police officers assigned to patrol participated in this study. The preference for patrol officers is reasonable for the purposes of the study as patrol officers are more likely to come into close contact with citizens, have the opportunity to encounter situations in which ethical issues arise, and may make more ethical decisions than other officers. A survey questionnaire was used as the data collection method.

The findings showed that the majority of respondents had positive attitudes toward their professional ethics and felt certain about most ethical standards prescribed in the Code of Ethics. For example, 63 percent reported their intention to take some action if they were aware of a fellow officers' unethical conduct. However, the questionnaire did not utilize various types of unethical conduct that could have shown differences in a respondent's response to a range of unethical behaviors. On the other hand, a considerable number of respondents indicated lack of clarity, reliance on individual ethical considerations in situations where the Code of Ethics was not clear, and intentions to utilize methods outside their professional ethics. For example, 16 percent said that they would probably utilize illegal means for apprehension of a criminal when no legal means were available. Another 36 percent agreed that "a police officer must sometimes use unethical means to accomplish enforcement of the law" (Felkenes, 1984, p. 216).

In an international study, Krejei, Kvapil, and Semrad (1996) investigated the link between job satisfaction of Czech police officers, narcissism, and their attitudes toward professional ethics. A randomly selected 135 participants were solicited and a total of 121 officers responded to the survey questionnaire and returned it to the researchers. The correlational statistics used for data analyses found that job satisfaction was significantly and negatively related to unethical professional attitudes. Officers who scored low in job satisfaction demonstrated significantly more unethical attitudes than officers who scored high in job satisfaction. The correlation between job satisfaction and ethical attitudes was expected to be closer among police officers who scored higher in narcissism compared to police officers who scored lower. The analysis supported the assumption; and the relationship between job satisfaction and unethical attitudes was significantly closer among officers who had higher levels of narcissism than those who had lower levels of narcissism (Krejei et al., 1996).

Overall, these studies suffered from methodological limitations. Although a 72 percent response rate was attained in Felkenes' study, only 74 officers completed the questionnaire. This was a descriptive study in which police officers' attitudes toward the Code of Ethics were examined in a simplistic manner. That is, only univariate statistical techniques, such as measures of central tendency were used. No inferences were made and no hypothesis testing was performed. Despite these weaknesses, Felkenes' (1984) study was important because it may be one of the first empirical studies to investigate police officers' attitudes toward professional ethics.

The second study (Krejei et al., 1996) used correlational statistics to examine the association between the variables. The limitations of study are related to the use of bivariate correlational statistics, which can only show whether there is a statistical relationship between variables; however, the existence of the association does not confirm that these variables are causally related. There might be no association between the variables because no multivariate statistical techniques were used to control the possible effects of other variables, such as situational or organizational factors.

A study by Hyams (1990) that used multivariate statistical techniques investigated the influences of individual demographic and dispositional factors on police officers' attitudes toward professional ethics. The demographic variables included age, gender, tenure, rank, assignment, and education. The dispositional factors were narcissism and perception of role. Participants for this study were police officers and academy recruits (a total of 150) from several Southern California Police Departments and Police Academies. The administrator of each police department was asked to randomly select names of police officers from a list. Participants then completed a survey questionnaire and returned it to a secured box in the administrator's office which was reclaimed by the researcher. The instrument also was administered to academy recruits in their classes by the researcher while the Academy Director was present. Of 148 instruments completed and returned, 3 were not useful. The final sample consisted of 145 respondents, 43 academy recruits and 102 police officers (Hyams, 1990).

Both correlation and regression analyses were performed on these data. Narcissism was found to be significantly related to unethical attitudes; and it had the greatest impact on unethical attitudes followed by rank and role perceptions. Respondents with higher levels of narcissism were found to have more unethical attitudes than respondents with lower levels of narcissism. Arrest and apprehension role perception was significantly related to attitudes toward professional ethics. Officers who were arrest and apprehension oriented demonstrated fewer ethical attitudes than officers who were service and peacekeeping oriented. Somewhat weaker but similar relationships between the independent variables and attitudes toward police ethics also were observed among the academy recruits. Narcissism, in general, was the most predictive variable of the attitudes toward police ethics (Hyams, 1990).

This study suffered from serious methodological problems. First, the sampling methodology used in the selection of the academy recruits was not clearly explained leaving no chance to critique it. Second, the procedures used in data collection from both academy recruits and in service police officers potentially biased the findings. Potential sources of bias include the presence of the Academy Director during survey administration, and the requirement that officers return completed instruments to the administrator's office rather than directly to the researcher. Even though the researcher sought voluntary participation and promised to ensure the participants' rights to privacy, respondents of this study might have felt some sort of coercion in completing the instrument due to the methods used in data collection. These methods made the findings of the study questionable. Lastly, no independent tests of significance were performed to determine if observed differences between in service officers and academy recruits were significant.

A more recent study by Greene et al. (2004) surveyed the perceptions and attitudes of police officers regarding the Code of Ethics in the Philadelphia Police Department. A randomly selected group of police officers composed of 504 officers from the population of 3,810 Philadelphia patrol officers was surveyed. Researchers were interested in gaining an understanding of organizational cultural value differences among the 23 police districts in Philadelphia, and their relationship to negative police behavior measured through activities, such as citizen complaints, departmental discipline, and police shootings. The findings also were expected to depict the organizational culture in the Philadelphia Police Department as a whole.

Respondents' ethics scores were aggregated at the district-level and then applied to the official data regarding negative police behaviors collected from a larger sample of 1,935 officers. The findings showed that different district cultures exist within the Philadelphia Police Department and that, in part, accounted for negative police behavior. For example, officers working in districts where attitudes toward ethics were weaker were more likely to be involved in shooting incidents (Greene et al., 2004).

In summary, a review of literature about police ethics has shown that attitudes of police officers toward their professional ethics have not been examined with regard to peer reporting. It is important to understand to what degree police officers adhere to their professional ethical standards and how this relates to their peer reporting of unethical behavior. An individual police officer's attitude toward professional ethics may be related to peer reporting in different ways. For example, police officers may have varying degrees of sensitivity or support for the standards or mandates of a professional code of ethics, and this may influence their peer reporting behavior differently. Therefore, the absence of research on the influences of a professional code of ethics on ethical decision making creates a gap in the literature on this topic, which this study intends to address.

Researchers in the ethical decision making literature, in general, have viewed formal code of ethics programs as characteristics of an organization and investigated them as a potential predictor of ethical decision making and behavior. This study, on the other hand, takes a somewhat different approach to the study of code of ethics. It is an individual level perspective which seeks to investigate police officers' perceptions of police professional ethics and their relationship to officers' intentions to report unethical behavior. The researcher argues that whatever the orientation and purpose of a code of ethics is, whether to optimize the integrity of professional activities and prescribe right and wrong behavior or to provide some tangible basis for public trust or assurance, as long as the members of an organization do not adhere to and abide by the code, it will not achieve what it intended.

Although the Code of Ethics and the Code of Conduct have incorporated certain professional standards that emphasize compliance to departmental rules and regulations and that intend to aid police officers in making ethical decisions in situations having ethical aspects, there is little empirical research regarding police officers' attitudes toward their professional ethics. Thus, this study can reveal what police officers think about their professional ethics and whether and to what extent it predicts their decisions to report peer unethical behavior. Based on the knowledge and discussions above, it is expected that police officers with stronger attitudes toward their professional ethics would have higher peer reporting intentions than police officers with weaker attitudes toward professional ethics.

H8: The stronger the attitudes of police officers toward their professional ethics, the higher the police officers' intentions to report a peer's unethical behavior.

Organizational Factors

Significant others or referent others, which "include peers and management" (Skinner, Ferrell, & Dubinsky, 1988, p. 211) and reinforcement contingencies (Ferrell & Gresham, 1985; Trevino, 1986) have been posited and investigated as organizational predictors of ethical decision making and behavior. Trevino (1986) and Trevino et al. (2006) argue that the attitudes and behaviors of peers can affect individuals' ethical behavior in organizations and can serve as a model to make ethical/unethical decisions. Similarly, Ferrell and Gresham posit that "individuals learn from others who are members of disparate social groups, each bearing distinct norms, values, and attitudes" (p. 90). Trevino further argues that "an organization can influence the ethical decision making behavior of its members through specific rewards and punishments for ethical/unethical behavior" (p. 613).

Clearly, both Ferrell and Gresham (1985) and Trevino (1986) draw upon social learning theories in their rationales for including referent others and reinforcement contingencies as organizational factors in their ethical decision making frameworks. Therefore, a review of social learning theories is presented below along with the empirical findings from the ethical decision making literature. Hypotheses for referent others and reinforcement contingencies are provided in the end of the section.

Social Learning Theory

The origins of learning theories can be traced to the "laws of imitation" theory introduced by Tarde (1912) who argued that humans learn all behavior through associating with others and through imitation. Drawing upon this concept, Sutherland (1947) sought to address why some youths who lived in the same socially disorganized neighborhoods and experienced the same criminogenic environment became involved in deviancy while others did not. He assumed that human behavior is determined from intimate others or associates, such as families, friends, and coworkers. Therefore, to understand human behavior, the primary groups to which individuals belong to must be examined (Warr, 2001). He proposed early versions of his learning theory sometimes referred to as differential association theory in 1924, and 1934, and more systematic versions of it later in 1939, and 1947 (Sutherland, 1947; Vold, Bernard, & Snipes, 2002; Warr, 2001). The theory has nine prepositions, and they are summarized below.

Sutherland (1947) argues that like all other behaviors, criminal behavior is learned through interaction in a process of communication within intimate personal groups, especially parents, teachers, and friends. Individuals not only learn criminal behavior, but techniques for committing crime, and values, rationalizations, and motives for criminal behavior from definitions favorable or unfavorable to violation of law. The "principle of differential association," refers to the extent to which an individual is exposed to and learns definitions, such as rationalizations and values, favorable or unfavorable to violation of law. For example, the learning of criminal or unethical behavior occurs because an individual experiences definitions favorable to law violation in excess of definitions unfavorable to law violation.

In contrast, one can learn conventional behavior when she/he experiences conventional traditions or associates with persons holding conventional definitions, rationalizations, and attitudes in excess of unconventional ones. Also, the acquisition of a behavior varies according to the modalities of differential association and learning, which include priority, frequency, and intensity. To put it simply, if a person is exposed to definitions favorable to law violation at early ages, especially during childhood and for a long time, there is a high likelihood that that person will commit crime.

Sutherland's differential association theory has been criticized. These criticisms can be summarized as follows:
- Neither definitions of frequency, duration, and intensity, nor measurement of the concepts of conventional and unconventional definitions were clearly defined, making the theory untestable.
- The process of learning was not specified.
- The strong correlation between delinquent friends and delinquency has been the strongest evidence supporting the theory. But, the meaning of this finding has been questioned for a long time regarding whether an individual becomes delinquent after he/she makes delinquent friends or an individual becomes delinquent before he/she makes delinquent friends.
- The theory is not valid because not everyone exposed to criminal traditions or associating with criminal others engage in crime.

Sutherland's theory was revised and reformulated by Burgess and Akers in 1966, and by Akers in 1973 and 1985 (Akers & Sellers, 2004). Burgess and Akers (1966) extended the theory referring to it as "differential association-reinforcement theory" and attempted to explain the process of learning (Akers, 2001). They added the concept of differential reinforcement to the theory drawing upon the concepts of social psychology, such as operant behavior, which is "conditioned or shaped by rewards and punishments" (Akers, 2001, p. 192). Subsequently, Akers (1985, 2001, 2004) reformulated the theory and proposed his social learning theory to explain criminal and deviant behavior in general. He identified and specified the process of learning with four major concepts: differential association, differential reinforcement, definitions, and imitation. Only the first two components of social learning theory, differential association and differential reinforcement, are of concern of the current study because these two components are proposed to influence an individual's ethical decision making in organizational settings in the literature.

Differential Association:
Differential association refers to the extent to which an individual is exposed to definitions that are favorable or unfavorable to illegal or law-abiding behavior (Akers, 2001). Differential association occurs

through the direct interaction or association with others, such as friends, peers, and coworkers, as well as the indirect interaction or association with more distant reference groups, such as teachers, the law, and authority figures (Akers, 2001). The definitions favorable to violation of law might be positive approving illegal behavior, negative, disapproving the behavior, or "neutralizing" the behavior in the sense that it is "all right... or not really bad" to commit the act "justifying or excusing it" (Akers & Sellers, 2004, p. 86). These groups also present individuals with role models to follow and shape behaviors. Individuals look for role models among their peers to follow and shape their behavior accordingly (Akers, 2001; Akers & Sellers, 2004).

As adapted to ethical behavior, several researchers (Ferrell & Gresham, 1985; Skinner et al., 1988; Trevino, 1986) argue that differential association may be used to predict an individual's ethical/unethical decision making and behavior. In this vein, peer influence within police organizations, as discussed in the review of cynicism, places strong pressures on the members of police organizations (Alpert & Dunham, 1997). Police officers, through the direct association and interaction with other police officers engaging in certain kinds of behavior as well as exposure to different patterns of norms and attitudes through this association, can learn certain behaviors, rationalizations, and excuses for actions that violate departmental rules and ethical standards. This, in turn, will influence their ethical decision making about situations that arise within police organizations and violate certain rules and standards.

Differential Reinforcement:
Building upon the concept of "operant conditioning" proposed by Skinner (1953), social learning theory explains how people learn through differential reinforcement. "Operant conditioning" theory assumes that behavior can be learned and reinforced by observing consequences (rewards and punishments) that follow the behavior. Social learning theory argues that people learn and condition their behavior not only through observing the actual consequences, but also through the anticipated consequences that follow the behavior (Akers, 2001; Vold et al., 2002). For example, Bandura (1969) argues "virtually all learning phenomena resulting from direct experiences can occur on a vicarious basis through observation of other persons' behavior and its consequences for them" (p. 118). Expected or

anticipated future rewards or punishments for a behavior will condition an individual's behavior because people tend to avoid behaviors that are anticipated to receive punishments, but tend to engage in behaviors that are anticipated to receive rewards (Akers & Sellers, 2004).

As it applies to ethical decision making and behavior, reinforcement contingencies (rewards and punishment) may predict an individual's ethical decision making within organizations. Trevino (1986) argues that organizations can increase ethical decision making among their members through specific rewards and punishments for ethical/unethical behavior allowing them to know what will be punished or rewarded.

Empirical Findings:
A number of studies have investigated referent others and reinforcement contingencies as organizational factors in the ethical decision making literature. Studies have generally found that referent others and rewards and sanctions are related to individual ethical decision making and behavior in organizations. For example, while sanctioning unethical behavior appears to positively influence ethical decision making and behavior, rewarding unethical behavior increases unethical behavior (Loe et al., 2000; Trevino & Youngblood, 1990). Peer influence also has been found to be related to ethical decision making and behavior in organizations (O'Fallon & Butterfield, 2005). A summary of the major empirical findings in studies regarding the influences of these social learning variables in ethical decision making is presented in Table 2 and Table 3.

Table 2

Organizational Factors: Significant Others

Year /Author	Sample	Method	Major Findings
1961 Baumhart	1700 Journal subscribers	Questionnaire	Peers influence ethical decision making.
1979 Zey-Ferrell, Weaver, & Ferrell	280 Marketing managers	Questionnaire	Perceptions of peer behavior influenced an individual's unethical behavior more than own belief.
1982 Zey-Ferrell & Ferrell	225 Managers	Questionnaire	Perceptions of peer behavior were the best predictor of ethical behavior.
1988 Izraeli	97 Israeli managers	Questionnaire	Perceptions of peer behavior were the best predictor of an individual's ethical behavior.
1989 Dubinsky & Loken	305 Salespeople	Questionnaire	Perceptions of peer pressure influenced individual ethical decision making intentions.
1993 Morgan	385 Managers	Questionnaire	Subordinates' perceptions of managers' ethics predict own behavior. Perceptions of managers' ethics are more salient to subordinates than to peers and superiors.

Table 2 Cont.

Table 2

Organizational Factors: Significant Others

Year/Author	Sample	Method	Major Findings
1993 Wahn	565 Human Resource professionals	Questionnaire	The more a person depends on significant others in the organization, the more likely the person will make unethical decisions and behave unethically.
1993 Zabid & Alsagoff	81 Malaysian managers	Questionnaire and vignettes	Perceptions of superiors' behavior had the strongest positive influence on managers' unethical decisions.
1994 Bruce	522 Municipal clerks	Questionnaire	Significant others had more influence on employees' ethical behavior than rules and code of ethics.
1994 Grover & Hui	248 college students	Questionnaire and vignettes	Anticipated reward had a significant effect on ethical decision making.
1994 Soutar, McNeil, & Molster	105 Australian managers	Questionnaire	Perceptions of others' behaviors were more influential on employees' ethical decisions than were ethical guidelines.
1996 Jones & Kavanagh	138 college students	Questionnaire and vignettes	Peer influence was significantly related to behavioral intentions.

Table 3 Organizational Factors: Rewards and Sanctions

Year /Author	Sample	Method	Major Findings
1978 Hegarty & Sims	120 Graduate students	Experiment	Ethical decision making was lower under conditions of extrinsic reward but higher under threat of punishment for unethical behavior.
1987 Laczniak & Inderrieden	113 MBA students	Quasi-experiment and vignettes	Perceived threat of sanctions had the only significant effect on ethical decision making.
1990 Hunt, Kiecker, & Chonko	330 Advertising executives	Mail survey	Neither rewards not penalties influenced advertising executives' decisions in response to social needs.
1990 Trevino & Youngblood	94 MBA students	Experiment	Participants in the reward condition made more ethical decisions than in the control group. Anticipated rewards had an indirect significant influence on ethical decisions.
1993 Victor et al.	159 Fast food employees	Field survey	Anticipated punishment for an unethical behavior was not significantly associated with employees' intentions to peer report.

Table 3 Cont.

Table 3

Organizational Factors: Rewards and Sanctions

Year /Author	Sample	Method	Major Findings
2003 Beams et al.	106 Accounting students	Questionnaire	Perceptions of punishment were not related to respondents' intentions to engage in unethical behavior.
2003 Shapeero et al.	82 Accountants	Questionnaire vignettes	Perceptions of reward for unethical behavior were significantly and positively related to respondents' intentions to engage in unethical behavior.
1998 Tenbrunsel	75 Graduate students	Experiment	Individuals in the high incentive condition were significantly more likely to engage in unethical behavior than were individuals in the low incentive condition.
2006 McCabe, Butterfield, & Trevino	5331 Graduate students in U.S. and Canada	Questionnaire	Perceived peer behavior had the strongest effect on academic dishonesty. Perceived punishment was not associated with academic dishonesty.

According to social learning theory, peer association and rewards and punishments are two of the sources of unethical or ethical behavior. Empirical evidence regarding the influences of these variables on ethical/unethical decision making and behavior supports these assumptions. However, no study to date has examined the influence of peer association and reinforcement contingencies on an individual's peer reporting behavior. Therefore, this study investigates the influences of peer association and punishment for unethical behavior in peer reporting of unethical actions by a police officer.

Social learning theory postulates that associating with unethical peers will positively influence peer unethical behavior (Akers, 2001). Guided by SLT, this study proposes that peer association also may influence individuals' ethical decisions with regard to peer reporting of unethical behavior. More specifically, associating with peers involved in unethical behavior is expected to negatively influence police officers' ethical decision making with regard to peer reporting.

H9: Police officers who associate with deviant peers are less likely to have intentions to peer report.

Social learning theory postulates that individual behavior is reinforced as a result of anticipated outcomes (rewards or punishment) that follow the behavior. As the empirical findings have demonstrated, while anticipated reward for an unethical behavior increases the possibility of unethical decision making and behavior, anticipated punishment for an unethical behavior increases the possibility that the individual will avoid the unethical behavior and increases the possibility of ethical decision making and behavior. Individuals tend to be involved in behaviors that are rewarded but refrain from behaviors that are sanctioned. Guided by social learning theory this study proposes that anticipated punishment for an unethical behavior also may influence police officers' ethical decision making with regard to peer reporting. More specifically, police officers who anticipate more punishment for an unethical behavior are expected to engage in ethical decision making more than officers who anticipate less punishment.

H10: Police officers who anticipate more punishment for unethical behavior are more likely to have intentions to peer report.

Issue Related Factors

As discussed previously, Jones (1991) made an important contribution to our understanding of ethical decision making when he introduced his "issue contingency" framework. It was not until Jones' work that the features of a moral issue and their influence on individual ethical decision making were considered. Since the moral intensity model was introduced, it has been extensively tested. In Table 4, a summary of studies about moral intensity and the major findings are presented.

Police Studies:
In the literature about police ethics, there are only a few studies that examined the link between issue seriousness and police officers' decision making. For example, Klockars et al. (2000) conducted a national study among police agencies in 1997, and investigated police officers' perceptions of departmental rules and regulations regarding police misconduct and their intentions to report police misconduct. They utilized 11 hypothetical scenarios depicting different forms of police misconduct ranging from minor to serious and asked a series of questions to measure police officers' perceptions of the issue seriousness and intentions to peer report for each scenario.

The scenario methodology has been the most widely accepted and solicited data collection method in the ethics literature in general (Butterfield et al., 2000), and in police ethics specifically (Ivkovic, 2005). In this methodology, several hypothetical vignettes describing various forms of unethical behaviors are presented to respondents and their opinions about each scenario are measured through a series of questions. Cavanagh and Fritzsche (1985) argue that ethical decision making components, such as ethical judgment and ethical intention can be best examined through vignette methodology. The vignette methodology allows researchers to design realistic yet ethically ambiguous situations to which respondents can respond (Butterfield et al., 2000).

Table 4

Situational Factors: Moral Intensity

Year /Author	Sample	Method	Major Findings
1985 Miceli & Near	8587 Randomly selected employees	Mail survey	Perceived seriousness of the wrongdoing was positively related to whistle-blowing intentions.
1996 Singer	160 Randomly selected managers	Cross-sectional. Mail survey	Magnitude of consequences, social consensus, and probability of effect were predictors of respondents' perceptions of overall ethicality of the ethical issues.
1996 Singhapakdi et al.	453 AMA members.	Cross-sectional. Mail survey	Moral intensity significantly related to respondents' behavioral intentions.
1997 Harrington	219 Information systems employees	Cross-sectional. Mail survey	Magnitude of consequences and social consensus had a significant impact on respondents' ethical decisions.
1998 Singer et al.	53 Employees	Survey questionnaire	Magnitude of consequences was a predictor of whistle-blowing intentions.
2000 Butterfield, Trevino, & Weaver	291 Intelligence practitioners	Cross-sectional. Mail survey	Magnitude of consequences and social consensus were predictors of moral recognition.

Table 4 Cont.

Table 4

Situational Factors: Moral Intensity

Year /Author	Sample	Method	Major Findings
2000 Flannery & May	139 Members of Metal Finishers	Cross-sectional. Mail survey.	Magnitude of consequences had a significant and positive influence on ethical decision making.
2001 Barnett	67 College students	Cross-sectional. Survey questionnaire	Social consensus and magnitude of consequences were predictors of respondents' ethical decisions.
2002 May & Pauli	189 Voluntary college students	Cross-sectional. Survey questionnaire.	Magnitude of consequences, social consensus, and concentration of effect had a positive and significant influence on ethical decision making intentions.
2002 Paolillo & Vitell	235 Business managers.	Cross-sectional. Mail survey with 2 vignettes.	Moral intensity had a positive and significant influence on ethical decision making intentions.
2004 Barnett & Valentine	373 Salespeople	Cross-sectional. Mail survey.	Magnitude of consequences had significant influence on ethical decision making intentions.
2006 Leitsch	110 Voluntary college students	Cross-sectional. Survey questionnaire.	Moral intensity dimensions were significant predictors of respondents' behavioral intentions.

A convenience sample of 3,235 police officers from 30 police agencies was solicited in the Klockars et al. (2000) study. The sampling methodology posed limitations to the external validity of the findings as the sample was not randomly selected and was not representative of the police population. Additionally, the study was descriptive in nature; no explanatory analyses were performed to predict police officers' perceptions of police misconduct and intentions to peer report. However, this study is important in the field of police integrity and has been replicated internationally in more than 10 countries (i.e, Ekenvall, 2002; Huberts, Lamboo, & Punch, 2003).

The study's findings are consistent with the findings regarding issue related factors presented in Table 4 above. For example, the majority of police officers indicated an increased level of peer reporting intentions in situations having higher levels of magnitude of consequences (for example, stealing from a burglary scene) than in situations having lower levels of magnitude of consequences (for example, accepting free gifts). Raines (2006) reexamined the Klockars et al. (2000) data to predict police officers' peer reporting intentions through multiple regression analysis. The findings showed that the seriousness of the ethical issues had the strongest positive influence on police officers' peer reporting intentions.

In another study, Rothwell and Baldwin (2007) surveyed a randomly selected sample composed of 300 police officers in the state of Georgia to predict police officers' intentions to whistle-blow on police misconduct. The instrument included seven different forms of police unethical behavior borrowed from the Klockars et al. (2000) study. Magnitude of consequences was measured through responses to scenarios depicting situations that included major policy violations, misdemeanors, and felony cases. The researchers assumed that magnitude of consequences would be high, and that it would elicit more peer reporting intentions in major violations and felonies than in misdemeanor situations. The analyses showed that police officers were more willing to report situations with greater magnitude of consequences. For example, the officers expressed more peer reporting intentions for major violations than for minor violations and more intended to report felonies than misdemeanors.

In a cross-cultural study, Ivkovic (2005) examined the survey data collected from 649 police officers from Croatia, 378 from Finland, and 3,235 from the USA and compared their perceptions regarding the issue seriousness on police misconduct. While a stratified random sample selection method was used for the Croatian police, convenience sampling was used for the Finnish and American police. Respondents were asked to evaluate the seriousness of the 11 police misconduct scenarios used in the Klockars et al. (2000) study. As a result of the analyses, the researcher concluded that police officers, although from different legal, economic, and political cultures, had a similar understanding of the issue seriousness of police misconduct.

The findings of this cross-cultural study should be interpreted cautiously as the researcher did not perform any tests to determine whether the three groups were comparable with regard to age, country crime rates, or agency size. In addition, the researcher did not control the influences of these differences on respondents' evaluations of the issue seriousness. Additionally, non-random sampling methodology limited the generalizability of the findings.

In summary, one of the purposes of this study is to answer the research question, what is the relationship between issue-related factors and police officers' ethical decision making. In this regard, this section of the literature review attempted to address this research question by reviewing the related literature. A review of previous studies has provided support for the Jones (1991) issue-contingent model of ethical decision making: there is a relationship between one or more dimension(s) of moral intensity and individual ethical decision making processes. That is, individuals were more likely to make ethical decisions in situations having higher levels of moral intensity than in situations having lower levels of moral intensity (May & Pauli, 2002; Paolillo & Vitell, 2002; Singer, 1996; Singer et al., 1998).

Among the dimensions of moral intensity, magnitude of consequences and social consensus have been consistently found to be the most important and significant predictors of individuals' ethical decision making (i.e., Barnett & Valentine, 2004; Butterfield et al., 2000; Harrington, 1997; Singer et al., 1998; Singhapakdi et al., 1996). The empirical findings regarding the link between the other dimensions of moral intensity and ethical decision making components were inconclusive due to mixed and inconsistent results (i.e., Barnett, 2001; Barnett & Valentine, 2004). Based on the results of the literature review above, in this study, the magnitude of consequences and social consensus dimensions of Jones' (1991) moral intensity have been chosen as issue-related factors likely to influence police officers' ethical decision making and proposed to influence their peer reporting decisions.

The Jones (1991) issue-contingent model has received a great deal of attention, especially in the areas of business and marketing ethics. A few studies have examined the influences of issue seriousness on police officers' decisions in the policing literature; but most of them are not based on clear theoretical grounds (i.e., Ivkovic, 2005; Klockars et al., 2000). This study proposes to fill this gap in the literature of police ethics by testing a model that includes the magnitude of consequences and social consensus dimensions of Jones' moral intensity theory. Specifically, this study investigates the influences of these factors on police officers' ethical decision making intentions with respect to peer reporting.

In his original work, Jones (1991) proposed that moral intensity dimensions would have a direct and positive influence on ethical decision making model components. Jones proposes that the dimensions of moral intensity will be positively related to individuals' ethical decision making intentions. Based on this knowledge and consistent with the empirical evidence from the literature review, the following hypotheses are proposed for investigation in this study.

H11: The greater the perceived seriousness of consequences of the unethical action, the higher the police officers' intentions to report a peer's unethical action.

H12: The greater the perceived social consensus that an action is ethically problematic, the higher the police officers' intentions to report a peer's unethical action.

CHAPTER 4

Roadmap to Research

RESEARCH QUESTIONS AND HYPOTHESES

Based on the review of ethical decision making theoretical frameworks in the literature along with a consideration of the whistle-blowing literature, five general research questions were developed for investigation of police officers' decisions to peer report.

1) What influences do individual demographics have on police officers' ethical decision making with regard to reporting a peer's unethical behavior?
2) What influences do individual dispositional factors have on police officers' ethical decision making with regard to reporting a peer's unethical behavior?
3) What influences do organizational factors have on police officers' ethical decision making with regard to reporting a peer's unethical behavior?
4) What influences do issue-related factors have on police officers' ethical decision making with regard to reporting a peer's unethical behavior?
5) Which one of the individual, organizational, and issue-related factors has the strongest influence on police officers' ethical decision making with regard to reporting a peer's unethical behavior?

The following specific hypotheses are offered to investigate the research questions presented above. The first six hypotheses listed test the influences of individual demographics on peer reporting.

H1: Older police officers are more likely to have peer reporting intentions than younger police officers.

H2: Male officers are more likely to have peer reporting intentions than female officers.

H3: Police officers who have more work experience are more likely to have peer reporting intentions than police officers who have less work experience.

H4: Police officers who are married are more likely to have peer reporting intentions than police officers who are not married.

H5: The higher the supervisory status, the higher the peer reporting intentions.

H6: There is no race difference among police officers in their peer reporting intentions.

The seventh and eighth hypotheses are offered to test the influence of police officers' dispositional characteristics (cynicism and attitudes toward police ethics) have on peer reporting intentions.

H7: The lower the level of cynicism, the more likely police officers will intend to report a peer's unethical behavior.

H8: The stronger the attitudes of police officers toward their professional ethics, the higher the police officers' intentions to report a peer's unethical behavior.

The ninth and tenth hypotheses listed are offered to test the influences of the organizational factors of referent others and reinforcement contingencies on police officers' intentions to report a peer's unethical behavior.

H9: Police officers who associate with deviant peers are less likely to have peer reporting intentions.

H10: Police officers who anticipate more punishment for unethical behavior are more likely to have peer reporting intentions.

The eleventh and twelfth hypotheses test the influences of the issue-related factors of magnitude of consequences and social consensus on police officers' intentions to report a peer's unethical behavior.

H11: The greater the perceived seriousness of consequences of the unethical action, the higher the police officers' intentions to report a peer's unethical action.

H12: The greater the perceived social consensus that an action is ethically problematic, the higher the police officers' intentions to report a peer's unethical action.

Data and Sample

This research project utilized secondary data analysis from a study originally conducted by Greene et al. (2004) on the Philadelphia Police Department (PPD). The data were publicly available and downloadable from the Inter-University Consortium for Political and Social Research (ICPSR) database. Also, permission was granted from two of the researchers of the original study to use these data (personal communications with Alex Piquero and Mathew J. Hickman, August, 9, 2008).

The researchers of the Philadelphia study collected three types of data. In the first part, official background and academy performance information of 1,935 Philadelphia police officers who were in the Philadelphia Police Academy between 1991 and 1998 were collected. The second part of the data was drawn from official PPD records and the Internal Affairs Unit regarding officer background, personnel data, and police negative behaviors, such as use of force, citizen complaints, and disciplinary action. The purpose of the Philadelphia study was to identify differences in academy performance and backgrounds relating to police problem behaviors, such as departmental discipline, physical abuse complaints, and police shootings. The researchers intended to improve the recruitment, screening, and monitoring processes within the PPD. Also, they sought to identify those officers who were at risk of negative behavior and to provide help to them (Greene et al., 2004).

In the third phase of the Philadelphia study, the researchers surveyed a group of police officers assigned to patrol in January 2000. The survey data included information about police officers' level of cynicism, attitudes toward ethics, and their perceptions of police unethical behaviors depicted in six different hypothetical vignettes (scenarios). The data were aggregated at the district level among 23 police districts in the city of Philadelphia and compared with the official data regarding negative police behaviors collected from a larger sample composed of 1,935 officers. The survey data were designed to investigate the police culture operating in the entire Department (Greene et al., 2004).

These data also were used in other studies to examine other issues. Hickman, Piquero, Lawton, and Greene (2001) used the data and tested Tittle's control balance theory on police deviance using data collected specifically for the purpose of operationalizing the control ratio. A study by Chappell and Piquero (2004) examined police deviant behavior. These authors employed Aker's social learning theory and attempted to explain the etiology of police misconduct measured through self-reported citizen complaints against the officer. In another study, Hickman, Piquero, and Piquero (2004) examined the validity of Regoli's (1976) modification of Niedehoffer's (1967) cynicism scale. Finally, Hickman (2005), examined the affects of cynicism on a number of police problem behaviors, such as use of force, disciplinary charges, and citizen complaints. These studies were discussed in the related section of this book.

The current study is unique in that it used data drawn from the survey phase of the Philadelphia study and investigated the influences of individual demographic and attitudinal factors, organizational, and issue-related factors on police officers' intentions to report another police officer's unethical and/or illegal practices or behaviors. The data were analyzed by combining scenarios in terms of types of behaviors. Three categories of scenarios, minor, moderate, and major scenarios were created to examine police officers' peer reporting intentions. Each category included two scenarios as they had certain similarities.

Descriptive Statistics of the Population and Sample

The population of the survey phase of the Philadelphia study included all Philadelphia police officers who held the rank of police officer, Sergeant, or Lieutenant assigned to patrol. There was a total of 3,810 officers from the 23 Philadelphia patrol districts. The researchers obtained a list of all patrol officers in January of 2000, from the PPD personnel database. A simple random sample of 504 police officers was selected from this list. Five officers refused to participate in the study, resulting in a sample of 499 available for analysis (Greene et al., 2004).

The sample of the Philadelphia study included a sample of randomly selected 504 officers from the population of 3,810 patrol officers. As previously mentioned, the final sample was comprised of 499 police officers. Table 7 shows the individual demographics statistics of the population and the sample as described by the original study. The original study did not record the participant's marital status, which is a variable of interest in this study and is noted in Table 9.

Descriptive statistics from the original study indicated that two-thirds (68.3%) of the respondents are male officers. The white and black officers are almost equal in their number. The average age in the sample is 35.14 years. The average number of years in policing is 7.46. The great majority of the police officers (91.2%) hold the rank of patrol officer. The majority of police officers are married (Married = 43.5%, Single = 39.9%). The descriptive statistics show that there are no major differences between the population and the sample characteristics.

Research Design

Experimental Design:
A cross-sectional survey design was utilized in the Philadelphia study. An experimental research design is not appropriate for the purposes of this study because experimentation is "a process of observation, to be carried out in a situation expressly brought about for that purpose" (Kaplan, 1964, p. 144). In other words, experimentation involves taking action or deliberate manipulation of an independent variable followed by systematic observation of consequences of the deliberate manipulation (Shadish, Cook, & Campbell, 2002). Experiments are appropriate for studying causal propositions and are well-suited to explanations and evaluation rather than to descriptive studies (Babbie & Maxfield, 2005).

Because experimental designs permit direct examination of causal propositions, Miceli and Near (1988) argued that this type of design is not appropriate for the investigation of an individual's whistle-blowing decision. Because of ethical concerns (e.g., equity in treatment, avoidance of harm, and right to privacy), researchers cannot randomly select members of an organization and place them into a manipulated unethical environment created within the organization and observe the influences of manipulated individual, organizational, and situational factors on individuals' whistle-blowing behavior (Miceli & Near, 1988). One of the most popular examples of this type of study is the "Stanford Prison Experiment" (see Haney, Banks, and Zimbardo, 1973).

Longitudinal Design:
A longitudinal research design is not well-suited to the purposes of this study because "longitudinal studies are designed to permit observations over an extended period" and to investigate change or stability in the nature of a problem of interest (Babbie & Maxfield, 2005, p. 97). Observations are made over an extended period of time on at least two

occasions to describe patterns of historical or developmental change and/or explain a causal relationship, especially separating the effects of age, period, and cohort (Menard, 2002). Menard discussed the features of longitudinal studies in greater detail and describes the shortcomings of this research design.

In brief, longitudinal studies are time consuming and expensive. Attrition or having subjects drop out of the study over time due to personal or other reasons, such as moving to another place or death, can occur and limit validity. Maturation, human recall, and time are other factors that challenge the validity of longitudinal studies. Participants' opinions might be altered by some specific events occurring during the study which potentially bias the findings. Menard concluded that "because of the differences in time, it is unclear whether the differences in findings reflect true changes or merely different biases or orientations on the part of the observers" (p. 36).

Miceli and Near (1988) argued that the primary reason why a longitudinal research design is unsuitable to investigate whistle-blowing is because to observe developmental changes in participants' whistle-blowing, they must be identified by name or by code to match the data collected at different times. This technique might cause individuals who are unwilling to identify themselves to refrain from responding to the questions or to give wrong information. They also contend that "only relatively clean organizations would allow researchers to investigate wrongdoing and whistle-blowing" through longitudinal research on whistle-blowing (Miceli & Near, 1992, p. 43). Because the issues of selection bias and unrepresentativeness of organizations are salient threats to the internal and external validity of longitudinal studies on whistle-blowing, Miceli and Near (1992) conclude that a longitudinal research design probably is not well-suited to the purposes of this study.

Cross-sectional Design:
Cross-sectional research design can be used to describe or explore a "phenomenon by taking a cross-section of it at one time and analyzing that cross-section carefully" (Babbie & Maxfield, 2005, p. 96). A cross-sectional survey design is appropriate when the purposes are to collect data on many variables from a large population spread across large geographical areas. Depending on the survey design, it can be also quick and relatively economical to collect these data (Bachman &

Schutt, 2007). Researchers are permitted to take an adequate and representative sample, such as a random sample from a population of interest, and investigate the current conditions and characteristics or some other aspects of the sample and make inferences to the population from the sample parameters (Patten, 2002). Conversely, in cross-sectional studies, it is difficult to establish a causal relationship between variables of interest (Babbie, 2001).

In conclusion, the purpose of this study is to investigate factors proposed to influence police officers' ethical decision making with regard to peer reporting and describe the process of police officers' peer reporting decisions. This study is not intended to describe developmental change in police officers' peer reporting decisions, nor is it intended to explain a causal proposition with regard to peer reporting. Therefore, neither experimental nor longitudinal research design is suitable for this study. Consistent with the ethics literature discussed in the previous chapter, a cross-sectional research design, which is the most widely used research design in ethics research, is preferred in this study, and the Philadelphia study is a cross-sectional study.

Data Collection Methods

In the ethics literature, researchers frequently use a survey questionnaire along with hypothetical vignettes or scenarios portraying various unethical situations as a data collection method (i.e., Klockars et al., 2000; Kohlberg, 1969; Randall & Fernandes, 1991; Rest, 1986). Individuals are likely to be unreceptive to direct observation of their ethical decisions and behaviors because of the sensitive nature of the topic (Trevino, 1986). A one-on-one interview methodology also is inappropriate because individuals would be reluctant to reveal their opinions due to the sensitivity of an issue like peer reporting. Therefore, a survey questionnaire along with a series of short vignettes depicting various forms of police unethical behaviors is the most appropriate data collection technique for this type of study.

Table 5 *Characteristics of the Population and Sample of the Original Study*

Variable	Population (N = 3,810) Frequency (Percent)	Sample (n = 499) Frequency (Percent)
Sex		
Male	2,720 (71.4)	341(68.3)
Female	1,090 (28.6)	158(31.7)
Race		
White	1,915 (50.3)	232(46.5)
Black	1,614 (42.4)	228(45.7)
Latino	238 (6.2)	31(6.2)
Asian	31(0.8)	7(1.4)
American Indian	8(0.2)	1(0.2)
Other	4(0.1)	0(0.0)
Rank		
P/O	3,418(89.7)	455 (91.2)
Sgt	302(7.9)	35 (7.0)
Lt	90(2.4)	9 (1.8)
Age		
Mean	35.22	35.14
(SD)	8.37	8.24
Min -Max	20 - 75	20-61
Years of Svc.		
Mean	8.04	7.46
(SD)	7.14	6.93
Min-Max	0-48	0-37

Scenario Methodology:
The use of scenario or vignette methodology has been the most common data gathering method used in the social sciences across a variety of disciplines (Butterfield et al., 2000; Chappell & Piquero, 2004; Piquero & Hickman, 1999). Cavanagh and Fritzsche (1985) contend that an individual's ethical decision making and intentions can be best examined through the vignette methodology. This method of data collection has been utilized in numerous studies in ethics research

and found to be appropriate (Barnett, & Valentine, 2004; Dubinsky & Loken, 1989; Jones & Kavanagh, 1996; Klockars et al., 2000; May & Pauli, 2002; Paolillo & Vitell, 2002; Pollock, 1998; Singhapakdi et al., 1996; Trevino & Youngblood, 1990). The scenario methodology has several distinct strengths along with some possible shortcomings that can be minimized if not completely eliminated. For example, several authors (Barnett, 1999; Butterfield et al., 2000; Hunt & Vitell, 1986) similarly suggest that researchers can design a variety of ethically involved real life decision making situations that would allow the respondents to become more involved in the situation in question and examine their ethical decision making and intentions. Also, scenarios can be designed to allow researchers to manipulate a variety of individual, organizational, and issue-related factors and examine the influences of these variables on individual ethical decision making. In a similar fashion, Klockars et al. (2000) argue that asking about police officers' actual behavior or the actual behaviors of other police officers involving sensitive issues suggesting poor integrity might arouse their resistance to respond to a questionnaire honestly. This would potentially bias the validity of the findings of a study. Hence, these authors suggest that by using a scenario methodology, ". . .it is possible to ask nonthreatening questions about officers' knowledge of agency rules and their opinions about the seriousness of particular violations, the punishment that such violations would warrant or actually receive, and their estimates of how willing officers would be to report such misconduct." (2000, p.3).

As discussed previously, magnitude of consequences, a component of moral intensity, has been consistently found to be positively related to an individual's peer reporting decisions (e.g., Klockars et al., 2000; Miceli & Near, 1992; Singer et al., 1998). Morris and McDonald (1995) suggest "the use of multiple scenarios in ethics research is preferable" (p. 719).

The Philadelphia study included six scenarios at varying degrees of issue seriousness. The activities depicted in the scenarios are prohibited in the police code of conduct and professional ethical standards (see Appendix B for the Code of Conduct and Appendix C for the case scenarios and the relevant IACP National Law Enforcement Standards).

To determine whether police officers' peer reporting decisions change according to the seriousness of consequences of the issue, scenarios having varying degrees of seriousness are necessary.

Therefore, six scenarios included in the Philadelphia study depicted another police officer's unethical actions at three different levels of issue-seriousness. The first two scenarios presented unethical behaviors at low-level seriousness, the next two presented unethical behaviors at mid-level seriousness, and the last two scenarios presented unethical behaviors at high-level seriousness (Greene et al., 2004).

The first two scenarios depicted actions of another police officer at low-level seriousness: (1) accepting meals and objects of small value from merchants on his/her beat and (2) accepting gifts from local merchants, restaurants, and bar owners on holidays. The next two scenarios depicted actions of another police officer at medium-level seriousness:(1) doing a favor for another police officer who was intoxicated while driving by transporting him/her home and (2) use of excessive force. The last two scenarios depicted actions of another police officer at high-level seriousness: (1) stealing a watch worth about two days' pay for the officer after a burglary of a jewelry shop and (2) stealing money equivalent to a full-day's pay for the officer from a lost wallet he/she found in a parking lot (Greene et al., 2004). The researcher of the current study assumes that as the level of issue seriousness increases, the seriousness of consequences also increases and it is associated with increased peer reporting decisions (see Appendix D for the survey instrument).

Despite its strengths, the vignette methodology has some shortcomings. The most serious problem associated with this data collection methodology is the possibility of socially desirable responses (Randall & Fernandes, 1991). Randall and Fernandes argue that ethics research is naturally vulnerable to social desirablity bias due to the sensitivity of the topics studied. Respondents might be inclined to give a well thought out or the best answer because of the sensitivity of the issue, such as peer reporting. Therefore, social desirability bias, the tendency for police officers to give answers in the desired direction, is a concern that must be noted in this study.

Various precautions can be taken to diminish the influence of social desirability bias on respondents' responses. Human subject protection techniques, such as voluntary participation and privacy protections of respondents, are suggested to minimize the social desirability bias although they do not completely eliminate the problem (Randall & Fernandes, 1991).

The data collection procedures used in the Philadelphia study minimized the social desirability bias to some degree. That is, the possible respondents were informed about the nature and scope of the study, such as any risks, harms, or benefits prior to completion of the survey. Respondents were informed that their names were selected from a list of all Philadelphia patrol officers, and that their participation in the study was completely voluntary, meaning they had the right to refuse to participate. In fact, five officers did refuse to participate. In addition, respondents were informed that the survey was a part of the larger project being conducted in the PPD about police officers' behaviors and attitudes and that the information obtained in the study would be only used for academic purposes (Greene et al., 2004).

The confidentiality of the respondents also was assured by the researchers through the instructions that appeared on the front page of the survey instrument that read:

> You were randomly selected to participate in this survey. Your name, badge number, district of assignment, and a random number are written at the top of this page. The random number also appears at the bottom of the first page of the survey. Please tear-off this cover sheet and keep it or destroy it... (see Appendix D for the complete instructions).

However, anonymity of the respondents, another method to minimize social desirability bias (Randall & Fernandes, 1991), was impaired in the Philadelphia study because of the nature of the administration of the survey instrument to the officers. That is, the research staff attended the roll-calls and administered the survey to the police officers before they went out on the street. This might be considered a limitation of the Philadelphia study. However, given the potential for a low response rate with mail surveys (Dillman, 2007), this type of data collection method might be a solution to a possible low response rate.

Other methods to reduce the social desirability bias are careful construction of the scenarios to accurately reflect details of the situations familiar to the respondents and the use of previously established and tested scenarios by other researchers whenever possible (Weber, 1992). As mentioned previously, the scenarios used in the Philadelphia study, were borrowed from the Klockars et al. (2000) study and have been used in many studies and in more than 10 countries. These scenarios have been found to accurately present realistic cases of police work and details of situations that are common to the police. In addition, the survey instrument was examined by an

Advisory Committee comprised of police officers from the PPD, members of the Internal Affairs Unit, and the Integrity and Accountability Office (Greene et al., 2004). Although these precautions minimize the social desirability bias, they do not completely eliminate it. Therefore, a measure of social desirability, which is commonly suggested as a control variable in ethics research (Weber, 1992), was used to investigate the extent of its influence on respondents' answers.

Survey Instrument

The survey instrument (see Appendix D) used in the current study has four sections and 83 questions in total. The first section contains the cynicism scale. Officers' level of cynicism was measured using Regoli's (1976a) modification of Neiderhoffer's (1967) cynicism scale comprised of twenty items. The second section includes attitudes toward the police ethics scale. Officers' attitudes toward police ethics were measured using the Krejei et al. (1996) ethics scale that includes fifteen items. The third section includes six hypothetical scenarios borrowed from Klockars' (2000) police ethics study. The respondents were asked to answer the same set of seven questions for each scenario. The final section consists of six demographic questions.

Data Collection Procedure:

Data were collected through a survey questionnaire during regular shift hours from police officers who were randomly selected from all Philadelphia patrol officers. To collect these data, the research staff obtained information about the shift schedule regarding which officers were scheduled to be at the roll-call. They traveled to all 23 Philadelphia police districts and attended roll-calls. A list of officers who were selected to participate in the study was faxed to each district before the research staff arrived at these roll-calls. The individual who was in charge of roll-call and who could facilitate the administration of the survey was contacted by the research staff upon arrival at the roll-call.

The research staff administered the survey to officers immediately after their roll-call, but before the officers left the station for patrol. It took four months to complete the collection of survey data from all officers selected to participate in the study. On average, it took 15 minutes for an officer to complete the survey instrument. Five out of 504 officers refused to participate in the study. The final sample was comprised of 499 officers. The officers were first instructed to read the consent form that provided information about the nature and scope of the study and they were advised that their participation was completely voluntary (see Appendix D for the consent form).

Measurement of Variables

Dependent Variable:

The dependent variable in this study is police officers' peer reporting intentions. In the ethical decision making literature, an individual's intention is generally measured with a single question that begins: If I were in the situation portrayed in this scenario, I would do (act, behave, involve)... In Table 6, a summary of the measurement of moral intent used in the previous research is presented.

Based on the data from the Philadelphia study, police officers' peer reporting intentions were measured through responses to the questions following each scenario. Consistent with the ethics literature, the specific question used to measure police officers' peer reporting intentions in each scenario was "Do you think you would report your fellow officer who engaged in this behavior?" The response categories were based on a five point Likert-scale option ranging from 1 (definitely not) indicating a low intention to peer report to 5 (definitely yes) indicating a high intention to peer report. In the current study, scores for medium, moderate, and major policy violations were summed to examine whether police officers' peer reporting intentions change according to the type of the ethical issues. Responses for each dependent variable could range from 2 (low intentions of reporting) to 10 (high intentions of reporting).

Table 6

Measurement of Moral Intent in Previous Research

Year /Author	Item	Response Categories
1989 Dubinksy & Loken	How likely is it you would engage in the behavior in each scenario?	Extremely likely Extremely unlikely
1996 Robin et al.	If you were responsible for taking the same action described in the scenario, what is the probability that you would make the same decision?	Highly probable Highly improbable
1996 Singhapakdi et al.	I would act in the same manner as the person did in the scenario.	Strongly agree Strongly disagree
2000 Flannery & May	What is the likelihood that you would continue to operate the treatment system as it has been for the last 30 years?	Extremely likely Extremely unlikely
2002 May & Pauli	I would release the findings… I would not release the findings …, if I were… It is likely I would release the findings…	Strongly agree Strongly disagree
2002 Paolillo & Vitell	I would act in the same manner as did the individual in the above scenario.	Strongly agree Strongly disagree

Independent Variables

The ethical decision making model developed for this study includes several individual, organizational, and issues-related factors as independent variables. Individual dispositional variables include cynicism and attitudes toward police ethics. Organizational variables include referent others and reinforcement contingencies. Issues-related variables include magnitude of consequences and social consensus. Individual demographics include age, gender, race, years of service, marital status, and rank.

Individual Demographics:
The literature review indicated that differences in individual characteristics may predict individual ethical decision making in general and peer reporting specifically. The demographic characteristics that this study examined include age, gender, race, and years of service, rank, and marital status. These variables also are included as control variables. Punch (2005) argues that control variables can be included to remove their confounding effects on the relationship examined because independent variables are somehow correlated with one another, and this can cause spurious interpretations of the relationships observed. The inclusion of control variables to a model allows researchers to accurately estimate whether and how a set of independent variables affect the dependent variable (Punch, 2005).

Table 7 demonstrates the measurement of the demographic variables in the Philadelphia study. To ensure ratio-level data, age and work experience in the PPD are measured through open-ended questions that ask years in number. Gender is measured as a dichotomous variable; supervisory status, measured through the officers' current rank is at the ordinal level; and race and marital status are measured at the nominal level.

Table 7 *Individual Demographics and Coding*

Your age	---------- (In years)
Years of service in the PPD	---------- (In years)
Your gender	Female = 1 Male = 0
Your race/Ethnicity	Black = 1 White = 2 Hispanic = 3 Latino = 4 Asian = 5 Other = 6
Your marital status	Single = 1 Married = 2 Separated = 3 Divorced = 4 Widowed = 5
Your current rank	Patrol officer = 1 Corporal = 2 Sergeant = 3 Detective = 4 Lieutenant = 5

Cynicism:
Officers' level of cynicism was measured using Regoli's (1976a) modification of Neiderhoffer's (1967) cynicism scale. The cynicism scale measured respondents' level of agreement with each statement through response categories which consist of a 5-point Likert-scale option indicating "strong disagreement" (1), "disagreement" (2), "neutral" (3), "agreement" (4), and "strong agreement" (5). In the current study, some items were reverse coded for the low scores to indicate a low level of cynicism and the high scores to indicate a high level of cynicism. A cynicism scale for each

respondent was created by summing responses for each item in the scale. The possible scale range was between 20 and 100 for respondents.

Neiderhoffer's (1967) original cynicism questionnaire consisted of a twenty-item additive scale designed to measure police cynicism as a unidimensional construct. All of the items in the questionnaire were incomplete statements. To complete the statements, respondents were asked to select one of the three sentence completion statements that, in their opinion, would make the incomplete statement correct. Three sentence completion choices included: a non-cynical answer scored as 1, a not so cynical answer scored as 3, and a cynical answer scored as 5 (Regoli, 1976a). One of the items in the questionnaire with multiple sentence completion choices is presented below.

The average police superior is _____.
a) Very interested in the welfare of his subordinates.
b) Somewhat concerned about the welfare of his subordinates.
c) Mostly concerned with his own problems.

Regoli (1976a) modified the format of the original cynicism scale and converted the response categories to a five-point Likert-type format. For example, Regoli changed the above mentioned item to read, "The average police superior is very interested in his subordinates." Half of the items in the scale ended with a cynical completion while the other half ended with a non-cynical completion. Respondents are asked to indicate their level of agreement with each item on a five point-Likert scale.

Researchers have attempted to replicate Niederhoffer's work since it was published and to analyze the reliability and validity of the cynicism scale. For example, Regoli (1976a) surveyed a group of police officers from nine different police agencies in the Pacific Northwest. A factor analysis (principle factors, varimax rotation) was performed to assess the dimensions of the cynicism construct. The analyses revealed that cynicism was a multidimensional construct having two to six dimensions. A five factor solution was selected "based on item's content, as to which dimension it best represented" (Regoli, 1976a, p. 133). These dimensions were: cynicism toward relations with the public, cynicism toward organizational functions, cynicism about police dedication to duty, cynicism about police and social solidarity, and cynicism about training and education. The analyses yielded an internal consistency score of .66 for the original scale consisting of 20 items.

The discussion about cynicism has important implications. First, rather than being one-dimensional, cynicism is a multidimensional construct. Second, a police officer can score higher on a certain dimension of the cynicism scale suggesting s/he is cynical toward that dimension while simultaneously scoring lower on the other dimensions of cynicism suggesting s/he is less cynical about those dimensions. However, because cynicism is not the main concern in the current study, police officers' scores on the cynicism scale were used as a general measure of their cynicism. In the original study (Greene et al., 2004), and in other related publications, such as Hickman et al. (2001) and Hickman (2005), the cynicism scale also was used as a general measure of police officers' cynicism. The current study adhered to this premise.

Attitudes toward Ethics:
Officers' attitudes toward police ethics were measured using the Krejei et al. (1996) ethics scale that includes 15 items. Items in the ethics scale are scored using a 5-Point Likert-scale ranging from strong disagreement" (1), "disagreement" (2), "neutral" (3), "agreement" (4), and "strong agreement" (5). Officers who score higher on the ethics scale are considered to have stronger attitudes toward police ethics than officers who score lower. The possible scale range was between 15 and 75 for respondents.

Peer Association and Reinforcement:
Using the same data from the Philadelphia study, Chappell and Piquero (2004) tested Aker's social learning theory to explain the causes of police misconduct measured through self-reported citizen complaints against the officer. Chappell and Piquero suggested that a new officer entering the job is exposed to differential association and learning within the peer groups in police organizations, which, in turn, influence the officer's subsequent behaviors. These authors argue that when social learning theory is applied to police occupational culture, police officers' behaviors are influenced by conventional or non-conventional definitions, attitudes, and rationalizations of other police officers within the peer groups.

They measured peer association and reinforcement through officers' responses to the questions regarding another police officer's actions portrayed in the hypothetical scenarios. The specific question that measured peer association was "How serious do most police officers in the PPD consider this behavior to be?" Response categories consisted of 5-point Likert-scale options ranging from "not at all serious" coded as "1" to "very serious" coded as "5." In the current study, the same measurement of peer association is used to test its influence on police officers' peer reporting intentions. A peer association score for each type of policy violation is computed by summing up the participant's responses to both scenarios in each type of policy violation. Scores for peer association variable could range from 2 to 10. The higher values indicate the perception of increased seriousness whereas the lower values indicate the perception of decreased seriousness for unethical behaviors. It is expected that decreased perception of peer attitudes toward unethical behavior is related to decreased ethical decision making with regard to peer reporting.

As discussed previously, reinforcement refers to anticipated rewards or punishments that will follow a specific behavior of others, which, in turn, is used as a reference by a person to condition his/her future behavior. Based on the assumption of social learning theory, the researcher of the current study assumes that police officers' perception of increased punishment for an unethical behavior depicted in the scenarios will be positively related to police officers' ethical decision making with regard to peer reporting.

Chappell and Piquero (2004), in their study, tested the influence of reinforcement on police unethical behavior measured through self-reported citizen complaints. The specific question that measured reinforcement was "If another officer engaged in this behavior and was discovered doing so, what if any discipline do you think would follow?" Response categories for this item ranged from none (1), to verbal reprimand (2), written reprimand (3), suspension without pay (4), demotion in rank (5), and dismissal (6). In the current study, the same measurement of reinforcement is used to test the influences of reinforcement on police officers' ethical decision making with regard to peer reporting. A separate reinforcement score for each type of policy violation is computed by summing the participant's responses to both scenarios in each type of policy violation. Scores for reinforcement variable could range from 2 to 12. The higher values correspond to greater punishment expected for unethical behaviors in the scenarios and are assumed to be related to increased ethical decision making with regard to peer reporting.

Seriousness of Consequences:
As discussed previously, the seriousness of the consequences dimension of moral intensity theory suggests that the intensity of an ethical issue will be higher if the ethical issue is more serious rather than less serious (Jones, 1991). In previous research, some researchers manipulated objective measures of moral intensity (Chia & Mee, 2000; Frey, 2000) while others used subjective measures of moral intensity dimensions (Flannery & May, 2000; May & Pauli, 2002; Singer, 1996; Singhapakdi et al., 1996). Other researchers used a single item (Barnett & Valentine, 2004; Leitsch, 2006; Miceli & Near, 1985; Singer et al., 1998; Singhapakdi et al., 1996) while a couple of researchers used multiple items (Barnett, 2001; May & Pauli, 2002) to measure the dimensions of moral intensity.

Based on these data, the seriousness of consequences of unethical actions depicted in the scenarios was measured through questions after each scenario from the perceptions of police officers. The specific question that measured seriousness of consequences was: "How serious do you consider this behavior to be?" The response categories consist of 5-point Likert-scale options ranging from "not at all serious" coded as (1) to "very serious" coded as (5). In the current study, responses to both scenarios in each type of policy violation are summed to calculate the participant's scores for each type of policy violation. Responses for peer association variable could range from 2 (low seriousness of consequences) to 10 (high seriousness of consequences).

Social Consensus:
The social consensus dimension of moral intensity theory suggests that the higher the social consensus that the issue is ethically problematic, the higher the moral intensity of that issue. Social consensus was measured through questions after each scenario. The specific question that measured the social consensus variable was: "Would this behavior

be regarded as a violation of official policy?" The response categories consisted of three options "Yes," "No," "Not sure" and were coded as 1 for "No," 2 for "Not sure," and 3 for "Yes" in the current study.

Reliability and Validity

There are four basic ways of assessing the reliability of social science measures: test-retest, split-halves, alternative-form, and internal consistency methods (Carmines & Zeller, 1979). Carmines and Zeller discuss these reliability methods in greater detail in their book and suggest that the first two approaches are not useful for estimating the reliability of empirical measurements due to their shortcomings. They recommended the alternative-form method but argued that it would be practically quite difficult to develop alternative forms that are parallel social science measures. Therefore, they recommend the internal consistency approach for estimating reliability of empirical measurements.

The internal consistency approach is used to estimate the reliability of the measurement scales in this study. Internal consistency simply means that there should be a high correlation among the items used to measure the same underlying concept. Internal consistency statistics describe the correlation among multiple items, which can be determined with Cronbach's (1951) procedure for coefficient alpha (Carmines & Zeller, 1979). The factor analysis method using principle component analysis with varimax rotation also is used to assess the dimensionality of the scales.

Analysis Plan

In this study, the Statistical Package for the Social Sciences (SPSS), version 16.0 for Windows, was used to conduct all data analysis. Various statistical techniques at different levels were used to achieve the purposes of this study.

At the univariate level, descriptive statistics were computed for each of the study variables. Descriptive statistics reduce and summarize data and organize data into a useful form to demonstrate general information about characteristics of a sample or a population (Bachman

& Paternoster, 2004). Descriptive statistics generate two different statistics: measures of central tendency (e.g., mean, median, and mode) and measures of dispersion (e.g., standard deviation). Measures of central tendency and dispersion and other descriptive statistics were calculated to investigate the study variables.

At the bivariate level, bivariate statistical techniques were used to investigate the study variables. Pearson correlations between all study variables were calculated to investigate the magnitude and direction of the relationship among all of the variables of the study and to assist in determining if any of the independent variables are highly correlated with each other.

At the multivariate level, multiple regression statistical techniques were used to test the research hypotheses and investigate the relative influences of the study variables on peer reporting. Multiple regression is an advanced correlational technique that allows researchers to assess whether and how the independent variables entered in the model influence the dependent variable (Patten, 2002). In the current study, a standard multiple regression was used to estimate the extent to which each of the study variables influence police officers' peer reporting intentions while controlling for the influences of the other variables inserted in the regression model. The following equation illustrates the full regression model that is used to predict police officers' peer reporting intentions.

$\hat{Y}_{(low, medium, high)} = \alpha$ + B1 (age) + B2 (gender) + B3 (race) + B4 (years of work experience) + B5 (rank) + B6 (marital status) + B7 (cynicism) + B8 (attitudes toward professional ethics) + B9 (peer association) + B10 (reinforcement) + B11 (seriousness of consequences) + B12 (social consensus) + ε

Where "$\hat{Y}$" is the predicted value for a police officer's peer reporting intention, "α" is the estimate of the Y-intercept, "X" is the known raw score value on the independent variable, "B" is the slope of the regression line, and "ε" is the representative of the errors of prediction.

CHAPTER 5

Empirical Findings

To test the hypothesized relationships among the variables of the current study, new variables were computed from the variables within the original data (See Figure 4 for all of the variables of the current study). First, items that were worded or coded negatively for the individual variables of cynicism and on the ethics scale in the original data set were reverse coded so that high values corresponded to a high level of cynicism and strong attitudes toward professional ethics. Additionally, new summated or composite scales for the cynicism and ethics variables were computed.

The independent variables of peer association, reinforcement, seriousness of consequences, social consensus, and the dependent variable of peer reporting also were computed in accordance with the three domains of unethical actions (minor, moderate, major) of police officers depicted in six scenarios described in the methods chapter. The individual demographic variables of marital status (coded 1 for married, 0 for unmarried), race (coded 1 for white, 0 for other), rank (coded 1 for supervisory status, 0 for patrol officer), and gender (coded 1 for male, 0 for female) were computed dichotomously because of fairly low frequencies in some categories within these variables (i.e., widowed = 3, Asian=7, Lieutenant=9). The descriptive statistics for the individual, organizational, and issue level variables as well as peer reporting, the dependent variable, are presented in Table 8 and Table 9.

Descriptive statistics indicated that the mean age of the respondents was 35 years, and approximately 58% of respondents were less than 35 years old. Police officers had an average of eight years of experience, and a majority of the respondents (64.8%) had less than

101

eight years of service. The majority of the sample (68.8 %) was comprised of male officers. The race variable indicated that 46.4% of the sample was white, and 53.6% was non-white. The sample respondents were primarily patrol officers with 90.5% reporting their rank as patrol officer. A majority of police officers were not married (53.7%). The disproportionate split on rank (427 to 45) truncates its correlations with other variables, but it was retained for analysis. Two of the other three dichotomous variables, race (247 to 214) and marital status (252 to 217) are approximately evenly distributed; gender (322 to 146) is not evenly split; it had approximately a 2.2 to 1 ratio.

Police officers' cynicism scores and ethics scores were computed by summing up the scores for each of the 20 cynicism items (range: 20 – 100) and 15 ethics items (range: 15 – 75). The actual lowest cynicism score was 35 while the highest score was 90. The mean cynicism score in the sample was 60.83 suggesting that this sample appeared to be in the moderate cynicism range. The lowest ethics score was 26 while the highest was 75, and the mean ethics score in the sample was 51.76, again in the moderate range.

Table 8 *Frequencies and Percentages for Dichotomous Variables*

	Variable	Frequency	Valid Percent
Gender	Male	322	68.8
	Female	146	31.2
	Valid (n)	468	
Race	Non-white	247	53.6
	White	214	46.4
	Valid (n)	461	
Rank	P/O	427	90.5
	Supervisor	45	9.5
	Valid (n)	472	
Marital Status	Non-married	252	53.7
	Married	217	46.3
	Valid (n)	469	

Table 9

Descriptive Statistics for Scale Variables

Variable	Valid (n)	Mean	Std. Dev.	Min.	Max.
Age	464	34.981	8.117	20.00	61.00
Years of Serv.	465	7.948	7.096	.50	37.50
Cynicism	474	60.829	7.683	35.00	90.00
Ethics	467	51.762	8.492	26.00	75.00
Seriousness of Consequences (Minor)	475	5.160	2.416	2.00	10.00
Seriousness of Consequences (Moderate)	471	7.513	2.197	2.00	10.00
Seriousness of Consequences (Major)	480	9.681	.925	2.00	10.00
Social Consensus (Minor)	469	3.277	1.105	.00	4.00
Social Consensus (Moderate)	456	3.653	.794	.00	4.00
Social Consensus (Major)	472	3.940	.386	.00	4.00
Peer association (Minor)	468	4.474	2.269	2.00	10.00
Peer association (Moderate)	466	6.665	2.155	2.00	10.00
Peer association (Major)	473	9.135	1.395	2.00	10.00
Reinforcement (Minor)	379	5.031	2.259	2.00	12.00
Reinforcement (Moderate)	395	7.172	2.490	2.00	12.00
Reinforcement (Major)	401	10.538	2.253	2.00	12.00
Peer Reporting (Minor)	458	4.388	2.365	2.00	10.00
Peer Reporting (Moderate)	457	6.017	2.457	2.00	10.00
Peer Reporting (Major)	463	8.127	2.155	2.00	10.00

Scores for each of the two dimensions of moral intensity (seriousness of consequences and social consensus) and organizational factors (peer association and reinforcement) were computed by summing each scale's items in accordance with three domains of unethical actions. The mean scores for the seriousness of consequences and social consensus dimensions of moral intensity show that police officers considered the third set of scenarios the most intense, and the first set of scenarios to be the least intense. That is, the mean scores of seriousness of consequences were 5.16 in the first set of scenarios, 7.51 in the second set, and 9.68 in the last set of scenarios. The mean score of social consensus was 3.28 in the first set of scenarios, 3.65 in the second set, and 3.94 in the last set of scenarios.

The mean scores for peer association and reinforcement also showed an increase from minor scenarios to major scenarios. The mean scores of peer association were 4.47 in minor scenarios, 6.67 in moderate scenarios, and 9.14 in major scenarios, suggesting police officers' perceptions of peer attitudes and behavior toward unethical behavior increased. The mean scores of the reinforcement variable were 5.03 in minor scenarios, 7.17 in moderate scenarios, and 10.54 in major scenarios, suggesting police officers' perceptions of punishment toward peer unethical behavior increased.

With regard to police officers' peer reporting intentions, the dependent variable, descriptive statistics illustrate that police officers appeared to have greater peer reporting intentions in major scenarios than the minor and moderate scenarios. That is, the mean score of peer reporting increased from 4.39 in minor scenarios, to 6.02 in moderate scenarios, and to 8.13 in major scenarios.

Exploratory Data Analysis

Prior to conducting a multivariate analysis, it is important to examine issues that are related to the quality of data that might, otherwise, result in incorrect conclusions (Mertler & Vannatta, 2005). Exploratory data analysis (EDA) is used to identify and fix or clean problems or errors in the data. Morgan, Leech, Gloeckner, and Barret (2007) outline the purposes for conducting EDA; (1) to examine the accuracy of the data (problems or errors with coding and inputting the data); (2) to deal with missing data; (3) to examine the effects of extreme values (i.e.,

Empirical Findings

outliers); and (4) to assess the extent to which the assumptions of a specific statistical procedure fit the data.

Descriptive statistics and frequencies were computed to assess the accuracy of data entry, missing data, and the distributions of the variables with respect to normality. For respondents 159 and 481, age appeared to be written as 3 and 5 respectively, and these were treated as missing because they seemed to be invalid. All of the other variables were within the expected range and identified as being coded accurately according to the codebook.

With respect to missing data, statistics showed that all of the variables had missing values for over 5% of the sample. Missing values when randomly scattered are less problematic than when non-randomly scattered because non-randomly missing values truncate the generalizability of the findings (Tabachnick & Fidell, 2007). Therefore, the patterns of missing data in all of the variables were examined using the SPSS MVA (Missing Values Analysis) function. The correlations with Little's MCAR (missing completely at random) test showed the probability that the patterns of missing cases deviates from randomness was greater than .05 in model 1 (p = .761) and model 2 (p = .476) but lower than .05 in model 3(p = .001). Because a statistically non-significant result is desired, MCAR may be inferred for model 1 and model 2 but not for model 3.

Therefore, the LISTWISE deletion method, which retains the maximum number of cases for analysis (Mertler & Vannatta, 2005), was utilized to delete the cases with missing values during the multiple regression analysis, leaving 318 respondents for model 1, 325 for model 2, and 341 for model 3. Cohen's (1992) power analysis test then was computed for each regression model to assess if these sample sizes are adequate to detect a medium population effect size (ES) of .15 or power of .80 at .05 alpha level. The power test indicated that the sample sizes of each of the regression models were adequate to achieve a medium effect size or power of .80 in a multiple regression analysis involving 12 independent variables.

To examine the distributions of the variables, the skewness and kurtosis coefficients were computed and histograms were visually inspected. The skewness and kurtosis coefficients should normally be between +1 and -1 to reach normality (Mertler & Vannatta, 2005). The variables age, years of service, peer association, reinforcement, seriousness of consequences, social consensus, and peer reporting had significant skewness and leptokurtosis and/or platykurtosis. The significance of skewness and kurtosis were estimated by dividing the coefficients by the standard error of skewness and kurtosis. Morgan et al. (2007) noted that in large samples most variables may be found to be non-normal because the standard error depends on the sample size. Similarly, Tabachnick and Fidell (2007) argue that in large samples (n > 100) variables that have significant skewness and/or kurtosis coefficients can be tolerated and these variables may not be divergent enough from normal to make meaningful differences in the multivariate analysis. Furthermore, "in regression, if the residuals plot looks normal, there is no reason to screen the individual variables for normality" (Tabachnick & Fidell, 2007, p. 82). Since this study involves multivariate analysis, all of the variables together were examined with respect to multivariate normality and outliers. The results of these tests are discussed in the following section.

Assumptions of Multiple Regressions

Multiple regression analyses are based on specific assumptions, and they are considered prior to data analysis. If the assumptions are not met, then the results may not be completely accurate and can lead to invalid inferences (Morgan et al., 2007). Therefore, it is important to examine the degree of fit between the data and the assumptions of analysis. However, the issue of meeting assumptions is a matter of degree, sometimes referred to as robustness, which suggests that a statistical procedure still can be used even if some of the assumptions of analysis are violated (Mertler & Vannatta, 2005; Tabachnick & Fidell, 2007).

Major assumptions involved in a multiple regression analysis include normality, linearity, homoscedasticity, auto correlation, and multicollinearity. Briefly, multivariate normality assumes that each variable and all linear combinations of the variables are normally distributed. The linearity assumption refers to a straight-line relationship between two variables in multiple regressions where these two variables can be combinations of several other variables. Homoscedasticity assumes that the variability in scores for one quantitative variable is approximately the same at all values of another quantitative variable. Auto-correlation assumes that residuals (differences between predicted and obtained values of the dependent

Empirical Findings

variable) are independent and not correlated with each of the independent variables. Mulicollinearity is a problem when some of the independent variables are severely or perfectly correlated ($r \geq .80$) with each other and contain overlapping information (Mertler & Vannatta, 2005; Tabachnick & Fidell, 2007).

To assess multivariate outliers, Mahalanobis distances, a measure of an outlier, were requested for each regression model and examined using chi-square (x^2) criteria at $p < .001$ and $df = 12$. Several cases were indentified to have Mahalanobis Distance scores greater than the determined critical value of 32.909 at $p < .001$ and were considered multivariate outliers. Mahalanobis distance cannot always give perfectly reliable results because it "is tempered by the patterns of variances and covariances" that can "mask a real outlier or swamp a normal case" (Tabachnick & Fidell, 2007, p. 74).

Therefore, caution was exercised by the researcher requesting Cook's distance statistics, "a measure of the overall influence of a single case on the model as a whole" and Leverage statistics (Hat-values), "a measure of the influence of the observed value of the outcome variable over the predicted values" (Field, 2005, p. 165). Any Cook's value greater than 1 can influence the model as an outlier. The average Leverage (the number of independent variable plus 1, divided by the sample size) can be between 0 (no influence) and 1 (complete influence) (Fox, 1991).

Stevens (1992) suggests that any score greater than three times as large as the average Leverage value is an outlier. The Cook and Leverage distance values were computed for each regression model. A Cook's distance value greater than 1 was not observed for any of the regression models. Several cases had Leverage distance scores three times larger than the identified cut-off points of each regression model ($\hat{h}_1 = .12$; $\hat{h}_2 = .12$; $\hat{h}_3 = .11$).

The assumptions of normality, linearity, and homoscedasticity were assessed through the examination of residual statistics and graphical examination of scatterplots, histograms, and normal probability plots for each regression model (Tabachnick & Fidell, 2007). With respect to normality, in large samples (e.g., $n > 100$), it is reasonable to expect that 5% of the residual scores lie outside ± 2 standard deviations of the mean and are distributed evenly below and above zero (Field, 2005). An examination of casewise diagnostics, histograms, and normal probability plots revealed that no more than 5%

of residuals had values outside of ± 2 limits in three models. Model 1 is normally distributed, and model 2 approximates normality. However, model 3 showed some deviations from normality. The examination of residual scatterplots and all partial plots showed that the assumption of linearity has been met in all three models. With respect to homoscedasticity, model 1 and 2 appeared to be approximating a rectangular distribution of residuals throughout the plot with concentration along the center satisfying homoscedasticity. Some deviations from homoscedasticity were observed in model 3. The assumption that residuals should not be correlated with each other was assessed through Durbin-Watson statistics for each regression model. The results indicated that there was no auto correlation detected among residuals in the three models.

Based on both Mahalanobis and Leverage distance tests, cases (#38, #60, #240, #259, #315, #318, #340, #373, #375, #441, & #479) were identified as outliers and were deleted. Then the distribution of the residuals was checked once again in model 3. The subsequent assessment revealed that no discernible improvements were detected with respect to normality and homoscedasticity after deleting the outliers. Therefore, these cases were retained for the regression analysis in model 3.

Multicollinearity was assessed through the examination of correlation matrixes (see Tables 10, 11, and 12). A .70 or greater correlation was detected between the variables of age and years of service in all three models and between peer association and seriousness of consequences. Therefore, caution was exercised by requesting the variance inflation factor (VIF) and tolerance scores for the independent variables. All of the models had independent variables with tolerance scores above the cut-off point of .2 (Menard, 1995) and VIF scores above 4 (Pallant, 2005). This indicates the absence of serious multicollinearity. Therefore, these variables were retained for analysis.

As a result of EDA, it was concluded that model 1 and 2 are fairly accurate models in predicting the dependent variable of police officers' peer reporting intentions regarding minor and moderate policy violations. Although, some improvements were achieved in model 3 with respect to normality and homoscedasticity, heteroscedasticity still exists. However, the presence of heteroscedasticity in this model is not likely to invalidate the findings (Mertler & Vannatta, 2005).

Table 10   Bivariate Correlations Minor Policy Violations (n=499)

	Variable	1	2	3	4	5	6	7	8	9	10	11	12	13
1	Age	1												
2	Gender (1=Male)	.109*	1											
3	Race (1=White)	.060	.270**	1										
4	Marital (1=Married)	.304**	.272**	.218**	1									
5	Years of Service	.712**	.254**	.224**	.293**	1								
6	Rank (1=Supervisor)	.278**	.138**	.215**	.177**	.408**	1							
7	Cynicism	-.063	.011	.033	-.006	.088	-.080	1						
8	Ethics	.062	-.085	-.124**	.022	-.098*	.051	-.329**	1					
9	Peer Association	.089	.049	-.015	-.015	-.055	.092	-.234**	.420**	1				
10	Reinforcement	.139**	.036	.061	-.055	.131*	.146**	.038	.162**	.203**	1			
11	Seriousness of Consequences	.134**	.052	.019	-.017	.034	.107*	-.193**	.509**	.753**	.229**	1		
12	Social Consensus	.033	.041	.173**	.012	.070	.130**	-.054	.158**	.099*	.306**	.218**	1	
13	Peer Reporting (1)	.155**	.090	-.024	.077	.083	.161**	-.216**	.514**	.578**	.209**	.664**	.146**	1

NOTE: ** p < .01, * p < .05

Table 11

Bivariate Correlations Moderate Policy Violations (n = 499)

	Variable	1	2	3	4	5	6	7	8	9	10	11	12	13
1	Age	1												
2	Gender (1= Male)	.109*	1											
3	Race (1=White)	.060	.270**	1										
4	Marital (1=Married)	.304**	.272**	.218**	1									
5	Years of Service	.712**	.254**	.224**	.293**	1								
6	Rank (1=Supervisor)	.278**	.138**	.215**	.177**	.408**	1							
7	Cynicism	-.063	.011	.033	-.006	.088	-.080	1						
8	Ethics	.062	-.085	-.124**	.022	-.098*	.051	-.329**	1					
9	Peer Association	-.014	-.034	-.123**	.045	-.133**	-.029	-.290**	.460**	1				
10	Reinforcement	.009	.121*	.042	.001	.062	.171**	-.102*	.186**	.307**	1			
11	Seriousness of Consequences	.028	-.136**	-.205**	.024	-.128**	.000	-.256**	.524**	.705**	.239**	1		
12	Social Consensus	.062	.093	.162**	.052	.097*	.062	-.115*	.177**	.227**	.330**	.329**	1	
13	Peer Reporting (2)	.065	-.074	-.179**	.041	-.067	.105*	-.252**	.520**	.573**	.229**	.678**	.143**	1

NOTE: ** p < .01, * p < .05

Table 12 *Bivariate Correlations Major Policy Violations (n = 499)*

Variable	1	2	3	4	5	6	7	8	9	10	11	12	13
1 Age	1												
2 Gender (1= Male)	.109*	1											
3 Race (1=White)	.060	.270**	1										
4 Marital (1=Married)	.304**	.272**	.218**	1									
5 Years of Service	.712**	.254**	.224**	.293**	1								
6 Rank (1=Supervisor)	.278**	.138**	.215**	.177**	.408**	1							
7 Cynicism	-.063	.011	.033	-.006	.088	-.080	1						
8 Ethics	.062	-.085	-.124**	.022	-.098*	.051	-.329**	1					
9 Peer Association	-.040	.032	.026	-.048	-.055	-.009	-.142**	.201**	1				
10 Reinforcement	.049	.017	.110*	-.039	.114*	.129*	-.043	.080	.301**	1			
11 Seriousness of Consequences	.024	-.040	.041	-.003	.029	.015	-.085	.155**	.545**	.305**	1		
12 Social Consensus	.061	.053	.068	.011	.044	.012	-.065	.055	.204***	.218**	.373**	1	
13 Peer Reporting (3)	.096*	-.051	-.052	.064	-.020	.119*	-.209**	.382**	.249**	.208**	.248**	.096*	1

NOTE: ** p < .01, * p < .05

Reliability and Validity of Scales

The reliability of scale variables was assessed through Cronbach's (1951) alpha coefficient (α), a commonly used measure for scale reliability (Field, 2005). Cronbach's alpha is concerned with the degree to which the items that make up a scale are internally consistent with each other (Pallant, 2005). An alpha value of .70 or above is an acceptable level for the reliability of a scale suggesting that all the items that make up the scale are measuring the same latent variable (DeVellis, 2003).

As discussed in Chapter II, the cynicism scale used in the current study has been subjected to reliability and validity tests in the literature since Niederhoffer (1967) introduced it. Consistent with previous research (e.g., Regoli (1976a, α = .66, n = 324), the cynicism scale reliability test for the current study generated a moderate reliability score of α = .67, n = 474.

In assessing the cynicism scale's validity, previous studies have suggested that the scale is multidimensional (Regoli, 1976a; Regoli et al., 1989; Regoli et al., 1990). In the current study, a principal components analysis with varimax rotation was performed to assess the structure of the cynicism construct. Consistent with the literature (i.e., Regoli (1976a; Regoli et al., 1989; Regoli et al., 1990), cynicism was found to be a multi-dimensional construct with seven underlying factors. In the literature, some researchers used an overall summated cynicism score as a general measure of cynicism level for a particular respondent (i.e., Greene et al., 2004; Hickman, 2005; Regoli & Poole, 1978) while others treated each dimension as a variable, such as cynicism toward supervisors (Regoli et al., 1990). As discussed previously, the cynicism scale in the current study was used as a general measure of police officers' cynicism levels.

The ethics scale consists of 15 items, and it has a good internal consistency with a Cronbach alpha coefficient of .83 (n = 467). A principal components analysis with varimax rotation revealed that items 3 and 15 did not load well with other items. However, the exclusion of these items did not result in a dramatic increase in the alpha score. In fact, only a .02 percent point increase was detected (.85, n = 471). Therefore, these two items were retained for analysis.

The reliabilities of peer association, reinforcement, seriousness of the ethical issue, social consensus, and peer reporting scales also were

Empirical Findings

assessed through Cronbach's alpha coefficient. Internal consistency scores for peer association, reinforcement, and peer reporting were .70 or above, with alpha scores ranging from .72 to .87. Internal consistency scores for seriousness of consequences and social consensus were .69 and .66 respectively.

Bivariate Correlations

Pearson correlation coefficients (r) were computed to describe the strength and direction of the bivariate relationships among the study variables and to assess multicollinearity. The results are presented in correlation matrixes in Tables 10, 11, and 12 in accordance with the three domains of unethical scenarios. With the exception of the variable of gender (male), which was correlated with the dependent variable in the unexpected direction in model 2 and 3, all of the variables' correlations with peer reporting were in the hypothesized direction. Independent variables that had significant correlations with peer reporting are discussed below. However, it is important to note that the bivariate results reported are limited to the strength and direction of the linear relationship between the independent variables and the dependent variable. Bivariate findings do not provide information as to whether and how these independent variables influence police officers' peer reporting intentions.

Of the 12 independent variables, eight variables in all three models were significantly correlated with police officers' peer reporting intentions. There was a statistically significant relationship between rank (supervisor), cynicism, ethics, peer association, reinforcement, seriousness of consequences, and social consensus variables and police officers' peer reporting intentions in all three models. Age was significant in model 1 and model 3 whereas race (white) was significant only in model 2.

As such, cynicism was negatively related to peer reporting; however, these were small size effects according to Cohen (1988). Social consensus had a positive correlation and a small effect size with peer reporting. Seriousness of consequences, peer association, and ethics had the strongest and a positive correlation with peer reporting in three models with correlation coefficient scores ranging from .39 to .68 at the level of $p < .01$. These were medium to large size effects. Rank (supervisor) had a positive and weak correlation with peer reporting in three models. Age was positively and significantly related to peer reporting in model 1 and model 3 whereas race (white) was negatively and significantly related to peer reporting in model 2.

Multiple Regression Analysis

A standard multiple regression was conducted using the 12 independent variables to further investigate the hypothesized relationships among the variables. Multiple regression analysis supersedes bivariate correlation analysis by allowing the researcher to investigate the influence of each independent variable on the dependent variable while simultaneously controlling for other independent variables. A separate regression model for minor, moderate, and major scenarios was computed. The regression results presented in the tables are discussed below with regard to the overall efficiency of each model, the absolute impact of each independent variable on peer reporting, and the relative contribution of each independent variable to the model in predicting police officers' peer reporting intentions.

Tables 13, 14, and 15 display the unstandardized regression coefficients or slopes (B), the intercepts, standardized regression coefficients or beta weights (β), and the multiple correlation coefficients (R), the coefficient of determinations (R^2) for each type of policy violation, minor, moderate, and major. The coefficient of determination, R^2, indicates the proportion of variance in peer reporting accounted for by the linear combinations of the 12 independent variables in the model. In brief, the R^2 indicates the model's predictive efficiency. The F ratio is a measure of significance for the model's predictive ability obtained by testing the null hypothesis that R^2 or all the regression coefficients in the equation equal zero.

The unstandardized slope is a measure of the absolute influence of each independent variable in the equation on peer reporting. The slope can be interpreted as the average change in peer reporting associated with a one unit change in a particular independent variable controlling for all the variables simultaneously. The null hypothesis for the regression coefficient tested indicates that that particular slope in the regression equation equals zero, and, that that particular independent variable has no significant influence on peer reporting practically. The beta weight is a measure of the relative contribution of each independent variable to the model in predicting police officers' peer

Empirical Findings

reporting intentions. The beta weight can be interpreted as the standard deviation unit change in peer reporting that results from a one standard deviation unit change in a particular independent variable in the equation.

Minor Violations (Model 1):
Table 13 illustrates the impact of all the independent variables on police officers' peer reporting intentions for situations involving minor policy violations.

Table 13 *Regression Coefficients for Minor Policy Violations*

Variable	B	Std. Error	β	t
Constant	-1.66	1.23		-1.28
Age	.02	.02	.06	1.09
Gender (1= Male)	.25	.22	.05	1.12
Race (1=White)	-.16	.20	-.03	-.80
Marital (1=Married)	.34	.20	.07	1.67
Years of Service	.01	.02	.01	.24
Rank (1=Supervisor)	.20	.34	.03	.58
Cynicism	-.01	.01	-.03	-.76
Ethics	.06	.01	.20	4.03***
Peer Association	.15	.06	.14	2.50*
Reinforcement	.05	.05	.04	.10
Seriousness of Consequences	.48	.06	.48	7.69***
Social Consensus	-.14	.01	-.06	-1.41
$R^2 = .57$				
$R = .76$				
$F = 33.88***$				

NOTE: *** $p < .001$, ** $p < .01$, * $p < .05$

According to regression results presented in Table 13, the linear combination of the 12 independent variables in model 1 significantly predicts police officers' peer reporting intentions $R^2 = .57$, $F(12, 306)$

= 33.88, p < .001. This model accounts for 57% of the variance in peer reporting. The F-ratio of 33.88 is statistically significant (p < .001). This finding indicates that the chance of committing a Type I error (rejecting the null hypothesis when it is true) that there is no relationship between the dependent variables and peer reporting is less than one chance in a thousand. Therefore, it is concluded that at least one of the slopes is significantly different than zero.

The multiple correlation coefficient (R = .76) suggests that there is a strong and positive linear correlation between the independent variables and peer reporting in the model. However, the coefficient of determination (R^2 = .57) provides a more powerful explanation for overall predictive efficiency in the regression model than the R score does. The model appears to be very efficient in predicting police officer's peer reporting intentions.

A review of regression coefficients reveals that only three variables (ethics, peer association, and seriousness of consequences) have a statistically significant and positive impact on peer reporting when controlling for the other variables in the equation. For example, a one unit increase in the seriousness of consequences resulted in a .48 unit increase in police officers' peer reporting intentions. The *t* value of 1.67 for the slope of .34 for marital status does not reach statistical significance. The researcher is not able to reject the null hypothesis at the alpha level of .05 in a two-tailed test. However, because a positive relationship between marital status and peer reporting is predicted based on past literature, a one-tailed test at the alpha level of .05 for this variable would produce a statistically significant slope as the *t* value of 1.67 is greater than the *t* critical of 1.65.

To further investigate whether a statistically significant difference exists in peer reporting scores for married and unmarried officers, an independent-sample t-test was conducted. There were no statistically significant differences in peer reporting scores for married (M = 4.62, SD = 2.60) and unmarried officers (M = 4.30, SD = 2.17; t (402.16) = -1.60, p = .11) in this model. The magnitude of the differences in the mean peer reporting scores was very small (eta squared = .006). Therefore, for this sample, it is concluded that marital status has no practical importance. This is evidenced in the small effect size.

The beta weights (β) indicate that seriousness of consequences has the strongest impact on police officers' peer reporting intentions, followed by ethics, and peer association.

Empirical Findings

Moderate Violations (Model 2):
Table 14 illustrates the impact of all the independent variables when regressed with the dependent variable of police officers' peer reporting intentions for situations involving moderate policy violations.

Table 14 *Regression Coefficients for Moderate Policy Violations*

Variable	B	Std. Error	β	t
Constant	.25	1.32		.19
Age	.02	.02	.07	1.19
Gender (1= Male)	-.04	.23	-.01	-.19
Race (1=White)	-.33	.21	-.07	-1.56
Marital (1=Married)	.05	.21	.01	.25
Years of Service	-.02	.02	-.06	-.98
Rank (1=Supervisor)	.62	.34	.08	1.82
Cynicism	-.03	.01	-.08	-1.90
Ethics	.06	.01	.21	4.26***
Peer Association	.06	.06	.06	.10
Reinforcement	.07	.04	.08	1.77
Seriousness of Consequences	.54	.07	.50	8.09***
Social Consensus	-.28	.14	-.09	-2.01*
$R^2 = .54$				
R = .73				
F = 30.29***				

NOTE: *** $p < .001$, ** $p < .01$, * $p < .05$

Regression results indicate that the linear combination of the 12 independent variables significantly predicts police officers' peer reporting intentions $R^2 = .54$, $F (12, 313) = 30.29$, $p < .001$. The multiple correlation coefficient (R = .73) suggests that there is a strong and positive linear correlation between the independent variables and peer reporting in this model. The coefficient of determination ($R^2 = .54$) indicates that 54% of the variance in peer reporting is accounted for by the variance in the 12 independent variables. In other words, the total amount of error was reduced by 54% when all 12 independent variables are simultaneously introduced into the model. The F- ratio of 30.29 for this equation is significant at the p level of .001. This suggests that the independent variables significantly combine to predict police officers' peer reporting intentions.

However, an evaluation of the slope coefficients reveals that seriousness of consequences, ethics, and social consensus significantly influenced police officers' peer reporting intentions. For example, a one unit increase in the seriousness of consequences resulted in a .54 unit increase in police officers' peer reporting intentions. The t value of -1.90 for the slope of -.03 for cynicism does not quite reach the t critical of 1.96 to reject the null hypotheses in a two-tailed test. Because a negative relationship between cynicism and peer reporting is predicted, a one-tailed test at the alpha level of .05 for this variable would produce a statistically significant slope as the t value of -1.90 for cynicism is smaller than the t critical of -1.65. Therefore, it is concluded that cynicism is statistically significant and negatively related to peer reporting in this model.

For this sample, the beta weights (β) indicate that the seriousness of consequences has the strongest impact on police officers' peer reporting intentions, followed by ethics, social consensus, and cynicism.

Major Violations (Model 3):
Table 15 illustrates the impact of all the independent variables when regressed with the dependent variable of police officers' peer reporting intentions for situations involving major policy violations.

Regression results indicate that the linear combination of the 12 independent variables significantly predict police officers' peer reporting intentions $R^2 = .25$, $F(12, 329) = 8.992$, $p < .001$. The multiple correlation coefficient (R) of .45, using all 12 independent variables simultaneously, indicates that there is moderate and positive linear correlation between the independent variables and peer reporting in this model. The coefficient of determination (R^2) for this model is .25 which suggests that 25% of the variance in peer reporting is accounted for by the variance in the independent variables. The F- ratio of 8.99 for this model is statistically significant at the p level of .001. The model significantly predicts police officers' peer reporting intentions, but the explained variation is lower than the explained variation in model 1 and model 2.

Empirical Findings

Table 15 *Regression Coefficients for Major Policy Violations*

Variable	B	Std. Error	β	t
Constant	-.39	2.01		-.19
Age	.04	.02	.13	1.93
Gender (1= Male)	-.10	.25	-.02	-.42
Race (1=White)	-.10	.22	-.02	-.45
Marital (1=Married)	.22	.23	.05	.96
Years of Service	-.03	.02	-.11	-1.43
Rank (1=Supervisor)	.50	.38	.07	1.34
Cynicism	-.03	.02	-.10	-1.84
Ethics	.07	.01	.27	5.62***
Peer Association	.06	.09	.04	.68
Reinforcement	.12	.05	.13	2.52*
Seriousness of Consequences	.34	.15	.14	2.28*
Social Consensus	.06	.33	.01	.18
$R^2 = .25$				
R = .45				
F = 8.99**				

NOTE: *** p < .001, ** p < .01, * p < .05

A summary of regression coefficients for this model indicates that the ethics, seriousness of consequences, and reinforcement variables had a significant and a positive influence on police officers' peer reporting intentions. For example, a one unit increase in ethics resulted in a .07 unit increase in police officers' peer reporting intentions. As Table 15 illustrates, the *t* values of 1.93 for age and -1.84 for cynicism do not quite reach the *t* critical of ±1.96 to reject the null hypotheses in a two-tailed test. However, a one-tailed test in the predicted direction for these two variables at the alpha level of .05 would produce statistically significant slopes as the *t* of 1.93 for age is greater than the t critical of 1.65; and the *t* of -1.84 for cynicism is smaller than the *t* critical of -1.65. Therefore, for this model cynicism has a statistically significant and negative influence whereas age has a statistically significant and positive influence on police officers peer reporting intentions. A one unit increase in police officers' cynicism score resulted in .03 unit decrease in their intentions to peer report.

A one-way between-groups analysis of variance was calculated to further investigate the impact of age on peer reporting with respect to major policy violations. The sample was divided into three approximately equal age groups (Group 1: 30yrs or less; Group 2: 31 to 38yrs; and Group 3: 39yrs and above) based on the cut-off points identified using the SPSS Visual Binding option. There was a statistically significant difference in peer reporting scores for the three age groups: $F(2, 441) = 3.10$, $p = .046$, at the p level of .05. A post-hoc comparison using the Tukey HSD test indicated that the mean score for Group 1 ($M = 7.80$, $SD = 2.30$) was significantly different from Group 2 ($M = 8.40$, $SD = 2.01$). However, group 3 did not differ significantly from either Group 1 or 2.

Despite reaching statistical significance, which is likely to be found with large samples like this one ($N = 499$), the actual difference in mean scores between the three groups was quite small. The effect size, calculated using the eta squared (sum of squares between-groups divided by total sum of squares), was .014. Thus, it is concluded that the difference between age groups in this sample has no practical importance. This is evidenced in the small effect size.

For this sample, the beta weights (β) indicate ethics has the strongest impact on police officers' peer reporting intentions, followed by seriousness of consequences, reinforcement, and cynicism.

Finally, a stepwise multiple regression using the backward deletion method also was computed to determine which of the 12 independent variables entered in the equation contributed significantly to the overall prediction of peer reporting. This was done separately for minor, moderate, and major policy violations. The results indicated that the variables that were found to be significant in standard multiple regression for each type of policy violation were again the only variables that significantly contributed to the overall prediction of peer reporting.

Statistical Summary

There are five research questions that this study aimed to address in regard to police officers' peer reporting decisions. To address these questions, twelve hypotheses were developed and tested through

Empirical Findings 121

standard multivariate regression models. The results of the multiple regression analyses are displayed in Table 16 and summarized below with respect to the research hypotheses.

Table 16 *Support for the Hypotheses by the Type of Policy Violations*

	Variable	Minor	Moderate	Major
H_1	Age	No	No	No
H_2	Gender	No	No	No
H_3	Race	No	No	No
H_4	Marital	No	No	No
H_5	Years of Service	No	No	No
H_6	Rank	No	No	No
H_7	Cynicism	No	Yes	Yes
H_8	Ethics	Yes	Yes	Yes
H_9	Peer Association	Yes	No	No
H_{10}	Reinforcement	No	No	Yes
H_{11}	Seriousness of Consequences	Yes	Yes	Yes
H_{12}	Social Consensus	No	No	No

Six hypotheses were tested to address the influences individual demographics had on police officers' peer reporting intentions. The first five hypotheses proposed that age, gender (male), years of service, marital status (married), and rank (supervisor) would positively influence police officers' peer reporting intentions across the three domains of unethical activities depicted in the vignettes. The sixth hypothesis stated that race would not be related to peer reporting. Despite the fact that all of these individual variables had relationships with the dependent variable in the hypothesized directions, multiple regression analysis revealed that none of these individual variables exerted a statistically significant influence on police officers' peer reporting intentions across three types of policy violations. These hypotheses were not supported by these data.

To address what influences individual attitudinal factors (cynicism and attitudes toward professional ethics) had on police officers' peer reporting intentions, two hypotheses were tested. As predicted, cynicism had a significant and negative influence on peer reporting in moderate and major policy violations. Ethics had a significant and positive influence on peer reporting across three types of policy violations. These hypotheses were supported by these data.

Two research hypotheses were tested to address the influence of organizational factors (peer association and reinforcement) on police officers' peer reporting intentions. As predicted, peer association was found to be positively related to peer reporting in that police officers who thought their peers considered unethical actions depicted in the scenarios to be more serious were more likely to peer report. Peer association was statistically significant in minor violations, but it was not statistically significant in moderate and major violations. Reinforcement had a positive influence on peer reporting across three types of policy violations, but it was statistically significant only in major policy violations. Police officers who anticipated more punishment for the unethical behaviors depicted in the vignettes reported an increased likelihood of peer reporting.

To address what influences issue-related factors (seriousness of consequences and social consensus) had on police officers' peer reporting intentions, two hypotheses were tested. The influence of seriousness of consequences was statistically significant and positive across all three policy violations supporting the hypothesis. As opposed to the hypothesized relationship, perceived social consensus had a significant and negative influence on peer reporting in moderate violations, but it was not statistically significant in minor and major violations.

The final research question sought to answer which of the individual, organizational, and issue-related factors had the strongest influence on police officers' peer reporting intentions. In the current study, the examination of beta weights indicated that the variables of seriousness of consequences, ethics, peer association, social consensus, and reinforcement significantly contributed to the models in predicting police officers' peer reporting intentions. In situations involving minor

Empirical Findings

and moderate policy violations, seriousness of the consequences was the strongest predictor of police officers' peer reporting intentions. Police officers' attitudes toward professional ethics were the strongest predictor of police officers' peer reporting intentions in situations involving major policy violations.

CHAPTER 6
Discussion and Implications

The purpose of this study was to investigate police officers' ethical decision making with regard to peer reporting. Drawing upon the most popular ethical decision making models proposed in the literature (Jones, 1991; Rest, 1984, 1986; Trevino, 1986), a peer reporting theoretical model was developed and tested using data from a random sample of Philadelphia police officers. The model featured three levels of factors that can influence police officers' peer reporting decisions: individual demographics, organizational factors, and issue-related factors. Simultaneously, the influences of police officers' attitudes toward professional ethics and their level of cynicism on their peer reporting intentions also were examined. In this regard, this study combined the individual approach, known as the "bad apple" theory, with the organizational approach, known as the "bad barrel" theory, in the study of an ethical issue in the policing literature. This chapter provides a discussion of the research findings, the policy implications, the strengths and limitations of the current study, and directions for future research.

DISCUSSION OF RESEARCH FINDINGS

The findings that emerged from the current study suggest that the main predictors of police officers' peer reporting intentions were individual attitudinal factors (ethical attitudes toward professional ethics codes and cynicism), organizational factors (peer association and reinforcement), and issue-related factors (seriousness of the ethical issue). These findings and variables that were found to have no significant influence on police officers' peer reporting intentions briefly are discussed below.

Demographic Factors

Despite the fact that the bivariate results from the current study found that some of the demographic variables (i.e., age, race, and rank) had a significant relationship with the dependent variable, none of the demographic variables achieved statistical significance in the multiple regression analysis. Thus, police officers' intentions to report another police officer's unethical activities cannot be explained or predicted in this sample by these demographic variables in this study.

Overall, these findings are consistent with previous research on ethical decision making. As discussed in Chapter II, an individual's age, gender, and work experience, in general, was not found to significantly impact individual ethical decision making (Brady & Wheeler, 1996; Dubinsky & Levy, 1985; Ford & Richardson, 1994; Izraeli, 1988; Loe et al., 2000; O'Fallon & Butterfield; 2005; Ross & Robertson, 2003). The absence of support for the hypothesized relationships between these demographic variables and peer reporting also is consistent with the inconclusive findings in the whistle-blowing literature (Dworkin & Baucus, 1998; Fritzsche, 1988; Miceli & Near, 1992; Rothwell, 2003; Sims & Kenaan 1998; Singer et al., 1998).

This study found that police officers' intentions to report another police officer's unethical activities are virtually unaffected by demographic differences. One potential explanation for the lack of statistically significant findings from the current study may be that once individuals become police officers and join the police force, their individual differences with regard to their intentions to peer report disappear. This also may be due to something unique about the police department and/or something unique about this particular sample which consisted of police officers only assigned to patrol duty.

For example, the police department's communication and enforcement of the professional rules and regulations may be related to patrol officers setting aside their individual differences and abiding by their professional ethical standards when police policies are violated by another police officer. Future research should consider examining the relationship between these demographic variables and peer reporting employing police officers assigned to other duties (i.e., administrative office duties) and in multiple police departments to allow for comparison.

Attitudinal Factors

The current study examined the influences of police officers' attitudes toward professional ethics on their peer reporting decisions. In the ethical decision making literature, the existence and/or enforcement of ethics codes as an organizational predictor of ethical decision making has been widely examined. The majority of these studies consistently found ethical codes to be one of the strongest predictors of an individual's ethical decision making within organizational settings (i.e., Barnett, 1992; Laczniak & Inderrieden, 1987; Trevino & Weaver, 2001; Trevino & Youngblood, 1990; Weaver & Ferrell, 1977).

Rather than the mere existence of an ethics code in the organization, the current study employed an individual approach and examined the relationship between professional ethics and peer reporting from the perceptions of police officers measuring their attitudes toward their professional ethics codes. This study was interested in police officers' attitudes and support for their professional ethical standards and how this was related to their peer reporting decisions when they were aware of a peer's activities that were in violation of the professional ethical standards.

The findings of the current study suggest that police officers' attitudes toward the police code of ethics were among the best predictors of their peer reporting decisions. Police officers who have more supportive attitudes toward professional ethics codes were found to be more likely to report a peer's activities that violate the professional ethical standards than police officers who have weaker attitudes. Furthermore, when major policy violations are considered, police officers' attitudes toward professional ethics were the strongest predictor of their peer reporting intentions compared to the other variables investigated. This finding has potential implications especially for police departments and administrators.

For example, given the significant association between ethical attitudes and peer reporting, police administrators should emphasize and consistently communicate the professional ethical codes and standards within the department. Continued ethical awareness training would assist in enhancing and maintaining police officers' levels of awareness about ethical issues in both the department and the community. Additionally, police administrators can consider rewarding ethical behavior among police officers to encourage ethical behavior and maintain an ethical environment within the organization.

Cynicism

Cynicism was another attitudinal factor used in the current study and found to significantly contribute to police officers' peer reporting decisions. As the literature review indicated, the police socialization process and the realities of police work are among the major sources of police cynicism (Crank, 1998; Niederhoffer, 1967; Sherman, 1982). Young officer assigned to patrol duty can develop cynical attitudes toward the police department and the general public they serve when they experience discrepancies between the ideal and the realities of police work and receive nasty treatment from the general public (Bennett & Schimitt, 2002; Niederhoffer, 1967).

Researchers have attempted to explain both the etiology of police cynicism and the consequences of it in the policing literature. For example, among the variety of individual factors that can affect police cynicism, the length of a police officer's service, was the strongest individual predictor of police cynicism (Lotz & Regoli, 1977; Niederhoffer, 1967; Rafky, 1975; Regoli & Poole, 1978). Lotz and Regoli (1977) also found as professionalism decreased, police officers' levels of cynicism increased. Regoli et al. (1989) examined cynicism as a predictor of job satisfaction among police chiefs. Police chiefs who were high on cynicism had low job satisfaction. Regoli et al. (1990) investigated cynicism as a predictor of job performance among police officers. Officers who are more cynical had poor work relations, higher arrest rates, and more hostile encounters with citizens than less cynical officers.

The current study, to the best knowledge of the researcher, is the first study that used cynicism as a predictor variable to investigate police officers' peer reporting decisions. The findings indicate that as police officers' levels of cynicism decrease, there is an increase in their peer reporting intentions. Overall, police officers who scored low in the cynicism scale reported an increased likelihood of reporting a peer's unethical activities than officers who scored high in the cynicism scale.

Discussion and Implications

This finding suggests that cynicism in police departments also has significant negative consequences with regard to peer reporting, in addition to lower job satisfaction, job performance, and poor work relations identified in the literature. Cynical attitudes lead to a reduced likelihood of reporting another police officer's actions and behaviors that are in violation of professional ethical codes, rules, and regulations within department. Development of cynical attitudes and behaviors can breed tolerance, also known as the "code of silence," among police officers for a fellow officer's unethical practices. This, in turn, can prevent police officers from reporting unethical activities occurring in the department.

Therefore, police administrators should be concerned with conditions and the socialization process that generate police cynicism which prevents police officers' reporting or revealing the unethical practices of police personnel. Future research should focus on exploring the sources of police cynicism, which have been found to be and continue to be a significant predictor of a number of police problem behaviors. Until the sources of police cynicism are identified and the reasons why police officers develop cynicism are answered, it is difficult to develop efficient policies and programs that can address these manifestations of police cynicism.

Although there is little research on the relationship between cynicism and ethical decision making in the literature, the finding of the current study is consistent with the findings of previous research (i.e., Anderson & Bateman, 1997; Detert et al., 2008). As discussed previously, these studies found a negative relationship between respondents' levels of cynicism and their ethical decision making. In general, individuals made better ethical decisions as their levels of cynicism decreased.

Organizational Factors

This study investigated the influences of peer association and reinforcement as organizational level factors on police officers' peer reporting intentions. As the literature review highlighted, drawing upon social learning theories (e.g., Akers 1973, 1985; Bandura 1969), ethical decision making researchers (e.g., Ferrell & Gresham, 1985; Skinner, et al., 1988; Trevino, 1986) argued that attitudes and behaviors of peers influence an individual's ethical decision making and behavior in organizations. An individual's behavior also is strengthened through the anticipated punishment that follows the behavior (Akers, 2001).

The examination of peer association and reinforcement variables and how they influence police officers' peer reporting decisions provided interesting findings. One of the most interesting findings is that peer association was a significant predictor of police officers' peer reporting decisions regarding minor policy violations involving accepting meals on duty and gifts of food and alcohol. Police officers' perceptions of peer attitudes toward these violations significantly influenced their intentions to report that behavior. Specifically, police officers who thought their peers considered minor violations to be more serious reported increased peer reporting intentions.

One explanation for this finding may be due to the fact that there is uncertainty among police officers as to whether these minor infringements are clearly against the police code of ethics. This ambiguity may cause police officers to consider what their colleagues think about the behaviors and how they might react to them. Therefore, their peer reporting intentions in these minor policy violations are shaped or influenced by their perceptions of peer attitudes toward these policy violations. This finding is consistent with social learning theory.

Despite the fact that the relationship was in the hypothesized direction, when moderate and major policy violations (i.e., stealing of cash or theft of an expensive watch) were considered, peer association was not a significant predictor of police officers' peer reporting decisions. These findings clearly indicate that when the policy violations become more serious or become worse, as in the cases of theft and stealing, whether officers would report their colleagues' behavior is unaffected by their perceptions of peer attitudes toward these unethical activities.

In the current study, model 3 includes behaviors that clearly deviate from professional codes of ethics. As statistical analysis revealed, these are the behaviors that police officers' are most likely to report. One explanation for these findings may simply be due to the fact that when a colleague's activities are obviously violating departmental rules and regulations, as well as being criminal, police officers do not care what their peers think about these behaviors.

With regard to the influence of the reinforcement variable, the only significant reinforcement variable concerns major policy violations and it is depicted in model 3. Although the relationships in model 1 and

Discussion and Implications

model 2 were in the expected direction, the reinforcement variable did not achieve significance in these models.

As mentioned previously, model 3 concerns behaviors that are clearly in violation of professional codes of ethics. Police officers, in general, anticipated the highest punishment (demotion in rank and/or dismissal) for the behaviors in model 3 whereas they anticipated less punishment for the behaviors in model 2 and model 1 involving minor and moderate policy violations. Police officers who anticipated more punishment for an unethical behavior are more likely to report that behavior. These findings are consistent with social learning theory.

Issue-related Factors

As discussed in the literature review, moral intensity theory proposes that the characteristics of the ethical issue can exert a strong influence on individuals' ethical decision making (Jones, 1991). A number of studies have examined and consistently provided evidence that moral intensity dimensions, especially seriousness of the consequences of the ethical issue and social consensus, are among the strongest predictors of individuals' ethical decision making (i.e., Barnett; 2001; Barnett & Valentine, 2004; Butterfield et al., 2000; Chia & Mee, 2000; Frey, 2000; May & Pauli, 2002; Miceli & Near, 1985; Paolillo & Vitell, 2002; Singer, 1996). Most of these studies were conducted in the fields of business and marketing ethics. The current study contributes to the literature by applying moral intensity theory, to the best knowledge of the researcher, to a police sample for the first time.

Perceived seriousness of the ethical issue and the social consensus dimensions of moral intensity were hypothesized to positively influence police officers' peer reporting intentions in the current study. The level of police officers' perceptions of the seriousness of the unethical activities depicted in the vignettes was found to have a significant influence on police officers' intention to peer report. It was the strongest predictor of police officers' peer reporting intentions in model 1 and 2, and it was the second strongest predictor in model 3. Police officers who perceived the unethical behaviors to be more serious were more likely to report these behaviors than police officers who perceived the unethical behaviors to be less serious. This finding was consistent with the previous research.

This finding implies that police officers consider and assign more weight to the intensity of the ethical issue when making ethical decisions than on the other individual and organizational factors included in the current study. When police officers are aware of the fact that an ethical issue is high on the moral intensity dimension, they recognize the seriousness of the ethical issue and intend to peer report.

No support for the effects of the social consensus dimension on police officers' peer reporting intentions was found in this study. Social consensus that the behaviors depicted in the vignettes are violating the professional ethical codes among police officers was only significantly related to moderate policy violations, but in the opposite direction. This was not consistent with most previous research. A negative but insignificant relationship also was observed in model 1 involving minor policy violations.

An important explanation for the lack of support for the social consensus dimension is that although the professional code of ethics (see Appendix A, B) clearly specifies that these behaviors are prohibited, it appeared that there is a lack of consensus among police officers regarding these behaviors. It may be for some police officers that behaviors depicted in model 1 and model 2 are trivial behaviors, not attracting their attention or consensus as to whether these behaviors are unethical. Another explanation for this unexpected finding is that there may be tolerance for these small infringements in the department in general, which could have influenced police officers' responses to these scenarios.

These minor infringements may be the most frequently occurring and the most widely discussed behaviors among criminal justice administrators, police scholars, and academicians. However, in reference to the "Broken Windows" theory (Wilson & Kelling, 1982), this "no one cares" and "no one is in charge" notion regarding these minor cases may be the explanation for the lack of social consensus as to the ethicality of these behaviors among police officers. Therefore, police administrators should emphasize the professional code of ethics and communicate to police officers that both minor and major violations are unethical and unacceptable.

Additionally, an effort through in service training or through informal discussion sessions can be made to increase police officers' moral recognition or awareness for ethical issues that are most likely to occur during patrol duties. Ethical issues that patrol officers are most likely to encounter should all be openly discussed, especially with young officers from the first few days they enter the police force. This focus would contribute to their awareness of ethical issues in police work and their moral reasoning development. In this way, they will be able to recognize ethical issues in police work and apply moral reasoning to these issues and make better ethical decisions (Rest, 1986).

Strengths

The current study contributes to the ethical decision making and the policing literature in this area in a number of ways. First, data used in the current study came from a random sample of Philadelphia police officers. Previous research about ethics in the policing literature had some drawbacks due to the sampling strategies utilized, such as a convenience and/or purposive sample (i.e., Klockars et al., 2000; Niederhoffer, 1967), and low response rates (i.e., Westmarland, 2005). These are among the serious threats to the external validity (generalizability) and the statistical conclusion validity (i.e., sampling error and regression assumptions) for the findings of a study. Consequently, the results obtained from a non-representative sample cannot be generalized or applied to the population from which the sample was selected.

As the methodology chapter highlighted, the researchers of the Philadelphia study employed a simple random sample selection strategy in obtaining the study sample. This was a fairly representative sample of the population from which it was drawn. Therefore, the findings of this study can be generalized and applied to all Philadelphia patrol officers.

The other strength of the current study was that although the current study involved secondary data analysis, the original data allowed the current researcher to be able examine factors that consistently have been found to be significant predictors of ethical decision making in the previous research. Some of these factors, such as cynicism and ethical attitudes, have not been collectively examined in one study. Furthermore, most of these studies have been conducted in business and marketing ethics. The current study investigated the influence of 12 different factors on police officers' ethical decision making with regard to reporting another police officer's unethical activities.

For example, the current study included two attitudinal variables, cynicism and attitudes toward professional ethics in addition to several demographic variables. Cynicism has consistently been proposed to influence individual ethical decision making and behavior in organizational settings, but it has been a focus in the ethical decision making studies only recently (Anderson & Bateman, 1997; Detert et al., 2008). The other attitudinal variable available within the original data was police officers' attitudes toward professional ethics. Previous studies have consistently examined the existence of ethics codes in organizations, but the current study examined the issue from the perceptions of police officers. The inclusion of these variables in the current study resulted in well specified models that yielded a 57% explained variance in peer reporting.

Limitations

Despite its strengths, the current study also has some limitations. One of the major limitations of the current study is that the original data were obtained from only one department, the Philadelphia Police Department (PPD). The examination of police officers' peer reporting decisions in one police department limits the external validity of the findings. Furthermore, the sample was comprised of police officers only assigned to patrol within the department. Consequently, the findings of the current study can be generalized only to patrol officers in the PPD. Replication of this study in multiple police departments of various sizes across the U.S as well as police officers of different ranks who are assigned to other duties would add to the generalizability of the findings.

Another major limitation of this study is that the original data allowed the current researcher to focus only on police officers' intention to peer report rather than actual peer reporting behavior. Although intention has been the main concern in most ethical decision making studies and the theoretical relationship between moral intent and moral behavior has been supported in previous research (i.e., Beck & Ajzen, 1991; Fishbein & Ajzen, 1975; Victor et al., 1993), the findings of this study may not be indicative of police officers' actual

Discussion and Implications

peer reporting behavior. Officers who stated they will report a colleague's unethical activity may not do so.

Another problem is that ethical issues like the ones in the original data would virtually provide different behavioral choices for an individual observer to act upon. First, a person can simply ignore the issue. Second, the person can choose to alter the behavior through advising his/her colleague or asking him/her not to do it. Last, the person can choose to report his/her colleague's unethical behavior. However, the original data allowed the current researcher to investigate only the measure of last choice (reporting) making the study limited to that measure among the above mentioned possible alternatives. On the other hand, this is one of the biggest drawbacks observed in the ethical decision making research. Therefore, in the future, ethical decision making researchers can consider measuring different behavioral alternatives.

Despite the fact that the original data provided well specified models for analysis, the regression models tested in the current study were limited to the variables available within the original data. The inclusion of some other individual level variables might have substantially increased the explained variance in peer reporting because none of the individual demographics had a significant effect on police officers' peer reporting decisions. Variables, such as education, ethical ideology, and moral development that were not available in the original data have been among the most significant individual predictors of ethical decision making in the literature. These variables are important, and they should be considered in future research. The inclusion of these variables would contribute to the knowledge regarding individual differences in police officers' ethical decision making.

Finally, the measurements of variables, such as peer association and reinforcement, had some problems. These organizational level variables are included in ethical decision making models based on social learning theories. The measures of these variables in the original data were limited to certain premises of social learning theory. For example, the peer association variable was measured only from police officers' perceptions of peer attitudes toward unethical activities. The other modalities of differential association and learning, such as priority, frequency, and intensity, and definitions were not measured. Future research should consider measuring these components of social learning theory to make a stronger argument that the theory provides a useful explanation for police officers' ethical decision making.

ORGANIZATIONAL IMPLICATIONS

The findings of the current study provide potential implications for police administrators. These implications are both proactive and reactive. Proactive implications include reducing the occurrence of unethical activities and maintaining an ethical environment in the department thereby reducing the need for peer reporting. Reactive implications are to encourage or increase intentions to peer report for police officers who observe the occurrence of unethical activities (Miceli & Near, 1992).

The current study found that one of the strongest predictors of police officers' peer reporting decisions was their perceptions of the seriousness of consequences of the unethical behaviors. This suggests the need for increasing police officers' perceptions of the seriousness of consequences of the ethical issues which, in turn, will hopefully influence their intentions to report the unethical activity. Perceived seriousness of consequences of the ethical issues can be improved through in-service educational and training programs. In these programs, police officers may be informed about the long term tangible and intangible costs of these ethical problem areas to the organization and the others parties involved in the situation.

Ethical problem areas that are most likely to occur in police work should be identified initially. The ethical vignettes used in the original study provide some indications of ethical problems on which police administrators should focus. Since Klockars and his colleagues first conducted the 1997 study, these vignettes have been widely used in a number of studies. However, these problem areas are not exhaustive because there have been a number of changes since then. Because of the emergent and unpredictable nature of police work as well as changes and developments in everyday life in today's modern society, police administrators should be cognizant of new and evolving ethical issues which police officers may confront. Such areas may include illegal activities (i.e., distribution of pornography and sexual exploitation or harassment) through the internet. Police administrators should focus on emerging problem areas that reflect contemporary situations that police officers will most likely face.

The reinforcement variable was another significant factor found in the current study. As discussed in the literature review, perceived punishment for unethical behavior decreases unethical decision making and behavior (Cherry & Fraedrich, 2002; Glass & Wood, 1996), but rewarding ethical behavior is the most influential method to support ethical decision making and behavior among the members of an organization (Trevino & Weaver, 2003). Thus, police administrators should consider placing more emphasis on rewarding ethical behaviors and continue disciplining officers who violated ethical standards to better communicate the importance of ethical behavior to officers in the department. More specifically, notwithstanding the type of policy violation, whether minor or major, a policy must be established that explicitly states that failure to report and/or condoning officer unethical activities will be punished or disciplined.

To increase police officers' perceptions of the seriousness of policy infringements, police departments should regularly accept citizen complaints regardless of the nature of allegation. These complaints must be carefully investigated and appropriate punishment must be imposed. Officers should understand that any type of wrongdoing is a serious issue for their organization. These efforts to maintain an ethical environment within the department also can encourage police officers' peer reporting intentions.

Failure to receive and investigate these complaints can convey a message to officers that the behavior is tolerated and acceptable, which may create a climate of leniency toward unethical behavior in the department. These activities can improve police officers' perceptions of the seriousness and the consequences of unethical activities and encourage ethical behavior. Ultimately, this would reduce the need for peer reporting.

The other important findings of the current study clearly indicate that peer attitudes toward minor policy violations influence police officers' intentions to report these behaviors while attitudes toward professional ethics codes influence police officers' intentions to report major policy violations. Because intention to report minor issues is shaped by peer influence, police administrators should focus more attention on these minor issues. To reduce peer influence, officers' knowledge and information about professional ethics codes can be increased through ethics training. These programs can be designed to further enhance police officers' attitudes and adherence to professional ethics codes and standards. The ethics training courses should start when officers first enter the police force and continue systematically throughout their career. Additionally, police administrators should consistently address these minor violations to develop consensus among police offices as to what constitutes policy violations and what behaviors are desired and expected from officers. Various activities and/or exercises, such as case discussions with police officers regarding questionable ethical issues most likely to occur may heighten officers' ethical awareness and enhance communication between supervisors and police officers. These activities may reduce the negative influences of peer association.

Finally, a study by Miceli and Near (1985) found that complainants' information about existing peer reporting channels and procedures is related to increased peer reporting behavior. As discussed in the literature review, complaint recipient is one of the dimensions of the whistle-blowing concept. Miceli and Near describe a complaint recipient as a person holding the power and authority to be able to take action and affect the action to make the desired changes. Thus, a complaint recipient and reporting procedures should be established within police departments so that officers who intend to report a peer's unethical activity are encouraged to do so.

Thus, within police departments, a body or a special division granted with the power and authority to receive and investigate complaints and able to take action to solve the problem must be created. Police administrators should explicitly and consistently require police officers to report peer unethical behavior. However, anonymous and confidential peer reporting channels or opportunities must be available for those who wish to report an unethical activity. These issues are critical to prevent reporters from retaliation, abuses, or other reactions by their colleagues.

IMPLICATIONS FOR FUTURE RESEARCH

There are several implications of the current study for future research. First, the findings of the current study are limited to only one large police department and to the population of patrol officers in the department. Therefore, future research could be conducted in multiple agencies of different sizes because police officers' peer reporting intentions would be different as the type of policy violations probably

Discussion and Implications

would differ in smaller jurisdictions. Additional scenarios depicting ethical problem areas for other assignment types (i.e., administrative and office) should be developed and applied to these work assignment groups to investigate whether peer reporting differs based on assignment type or rank.

The data used in the current study were obtained from a cross-sectional study. A cross-sectional research design can provide a snapshot in time for the phenomenon studied. Another method, a longitudinal study, would improve the findings of the current study. A longitudinal study may be conducted to investigate the influence of peer association on police officers' attitudes and behaviors. The policing literature indicates that the socialization process in the police occupation starts from recruitment and develops throughout the officer's career. A longitudinal study can allow future research to assess differences and changes in police officers' attitudes and behaviors toward violations of police ethics codes and standards. The results of a longitudinal study would also suggest additional organizational strategies both to reduce the need for peer reporting and to encourage peer reporting.

Future research about peer reporting should explore the influence of additional variables on peer reporting that have been consistently found to be related to individual ethical decision making in organizations in the literature. These variables might include ethical climate an organization, such as caring, benevolent, and instrumental (Cullen, Victor, & Bronson, 1993), individual variables, such as education level and cognitive moral development (Rest, 1986), and ethical ideology (Forsyth, 1980), and the relationship between a violator and a would-be peer reporter (Jones, 1991). Future research should explore the influences of these variables to expand the current findings about police officers' peer reporting decisions in police departments.

Finally, data collected through a survey questionnaire in the original study were the only data used in the current study. As discussed in the previous chapters, the self-reported information about sensitive issues like peer reporting may solicit socially desired responses to the questions. Although the researchers of the original study exercised cautions to reduce the influence of social desirability on study findings, officers who said they intended to peer report might not do so. Therefore, future research should collect additional data to substantiate and expand the findings of the current study. For example, departmental data about the actual incidences of peer reporting by police officers, citizen complaints about officer misconduct, and internal affairs investigations regarding officer misconduct can be used as supplementary data sources to better explore peer reporting in police departments.

CONCLUDING REMARKS

Unethical activities of police officers have enormous tangible and intangible costs to police departments; they affect the quality of police services, and the public's confidence in the police. In the ethical decision making literature, reporting colleagues' unethical or illegal practices is suggested as one of the preventive strategies for these unethical or illegal practices in organizations. However, the duty of loyalty to colleagues in police departments and the duty to report another police officer's illegal practices place police officers who witness these illegal practices in an ethical dilemma.

The duty of loyalty is a strong cultural norm among police officers that sometimes can result in an officer failing to report or turning a blind eye to another police officer's unethical and/or illegal activities. This is known as the "code of silence." On the other hand, the police code of ethics and standards requires police officers to report another police officer's illegal practices. Officers who witness a fellow officer's unethical and illegal practices have to decide whether they should report these illegal practices or remain silent. This is the dilemma investigated in this study.

For this purpose, a peer reporting theoretical model that included a number of individual, organizational, and issue-related factors was developed and tested using data from a random sample of Philadelphia police officers. The results that emerged from the current study provided interesting findings. For example, police officers' intentions to report peer unethical behavior cannot be explained by their demographic differences. The most important predictors of police officers' peer reporting decisions were the seriousness of the unethical behaviors and officers' attitudes toward policy violations. Peer association was influential when minor policy violations were considered whereas the reinforcement variable was influential when major policy violations were considered. A lack of social consensus on the ethicality of the minor policy violations among police officers also was observed. The findings that emerged from the current study suggested potential implications for police administrators who intend to promote ethics and maintain an ethical environment within the department. As discussed previously, these implications can help police administrators reduce the need for peer reporting and encourage would-be reporters who observe unethical behavior to report it. As in most social studies, the results of this study also revealed the need to expand the current knowledge and explore the influence of additional factors on police officers' peer reporting decisions.

APPENDIX A
Law Enforcement Code of Ethics

AS A LAW ENFORCEMENT OFFICER, my fundamental duty is to serve mankind; to safeguard lives and property; to protect the innocent against deception, the weak against oppression or intimidation, and the peaceful against violence or disorder; and to respect the Constitutional rights of all men to liberty, equality and justice.

I WILL keep my private life unsullied as an example to all; maintain courageous calm in the face of danger, scorn or ridicule; develop self restraint; and be constantly mindful of the welfare of others. Honest in thought and deed in both my personal and official life, I will be exemplary in obeying the laws of the land and the regulations of my department. Whatever I see or hear of a confidential nature or that is confided to me in my official capacity will be kept ever secret unless revelation is necessary in the performance of my duty.

I WILL never act officiously or permit personal feelings, prejudices, animosities or friendships to influence my decisions. With no compromise for crime and with relentless prosecution of criminals, I will enforce the law courteously and appropriately without fear or favor, malice or ill will, never employing unnecessary force or violence and never accepting gratuities.

I RECOGNIZE the badge of my office as a symbol of public faith, and I accept it as a public trust to be held so long as I am true to the ethics of the police service. I will constantly strive to achieve these objectives and ideals, dedicating myself before God to my chosen profession law enforcement.

APPENDIX B

Law Enforcement Code of Conduct

All law enforcement officers must be fully aware of the ethical responsibilities of their position and must strive constantly to live up to the highest possible standards of professional policing.

The International Association of Chiefs of Police believes it is important that police officers have clear advice and counsel available to assist them in performing their duties consistent with these standards, and has adopted the following ethical mandates as guidelines to meet these ends.

Primary Responsibilities of a Police Officer

A police officer acts as an official representative of government who is required and trusted to work within the law. The officer's powers and duties are conferred by statute. The fundamental duties of a police officer include serving the community; safeguarding lives and property; protecting the innocent; keeping the peace; and ensuring the rights of all to liberty, equality and justice.

Performance of the Duties of a Police Officer

A police officer shall perform all duties impartially, without favor or affection or ill will and without regard to status, sex, race, religion, political belief or aspiration. All citizens will be treated equally with courtesy, consideration and dignity.

Officers will never allow personal feelings, animosities or friendships to influence official conduct, Laws will be enforced appropriately and courteously and, in carrying out their responsibilities, officers will strive to obtain maximum cooperation from the public. They will conduct themselves in appearance and deportment in such a manner as to inspire confidence and respect for the position of public trust they hold.

Discretion

A police officer will use responsibly the discretion vested in the position and exercise it within the law. The principle of reasonableness will guide the officer's determinations and the officer will consider all surrounding circumstances in determining whether any legal action shall be taken.

Consistent and wise use of discretion, based on professional policing competence, will do much to preserve wood relationships and retain the confidence of the public. There can be difficulty in choosing between conflicting courses of action. It is important to remember that a timely word of advice rather than arrest which may be correct in appropriate circumstances-can be a more effective means of achieving a desired end.

Use of Force

A police officer will never employ unnecessary force or violence and will use only such force in the discharge of duty as is reasonable in all circumstances.

Force should be used only with the greatest restraint and only after discussion, negotiation and persuasion have been found to be inappropriate or ineffective. While the use of force is occasionally unavoidable, every police officer will refrain from applying the unnecessary infliction of pain or suffering and will never engage in cruel, degrading or inhuman treatment of any person.

Confidentiality

Whatever a police officer sees, hears or learns of, which is of a confidential nature, will be kept secret unless the performance of duty or legal provision requires otherwise.

Members of the public have a right to security and privacy, and information obtained about them must not be improperly divulged.

Integrity

A police officer will not engage in acts of corruption or bribery, nor will an officer condone such acts by other police officers.

The public demands that the integrity of police officers be above reproach. Police officers must, therefore, avoid any conduct that might compromise integrity and thus undercut the public confidence in a law enforcement agency.

Law Enforcement Code of Conduct

Officers will refuse to accept any gifts, presents, subscriptions, and favors, gratuities 01' promises that could be interpreted as seeking to cause the officer to refrain from performing official responsibilities honestly and within the law. Police officers must not receive private or special advantage from their official status, Respect from the public cannot be bought; it can only be earned and cultivated.

Cooperation with Other Officers and Agencies

Police officers will cooperate with all legally authorized agencies and their representatives in the pursuit of justice.

An officer or agency may be one among many organizations that may provide law enforcement services to a jurisdiction. It is imperative that a police officer assist colleagues fully and completely with respect and consideration at all times.

Personal/Professional Capabilities

Police officers will be responsible for their own standard of professional performance and will take every reasonable opportunity to enhance and improve their level of knowledge and competence.

Through study and experience, a police officer can acquire the high level of knowledge and competence that is essential for the efficient and effective performance of duty. The acquisition of knowledge is a never-ending process of personal and professional development that should be pursued constantly.

Private Life

Police officers will behave in a manner that does not bring discredit to their agencies or themselves. A police officer's character and conduct while off duty must always be exemplary, thus maintaining a position of respect in the community in which he or she lives and serves. The officer's personal behavior must be beyond reproach.

APPENDIX C

IACP National Law Enforcement Standards for the Scenarios

Scenario 1	A police officer routinely accepts free meals, cigarettes, and other items of small value from merchants on his beat. The officer does not solicit these gifts and is careful not to abuse the generosity of those who gave the gifts to him. **IV. A. 8 (a) Officers shall report any unsolicited gifts, gratuities, or other items of value they receive and shall provide a full report of the circumstances of their receipt if directed.**
Scenario 2	A police officer is widely liked in the community, and on holidays local merchants and restaurant and bar owners show their appreciation for the officer's attention by giving the officer gifts of food and liquor. **IV. A. 8 (a) Officers shall report any unsolicited gifts, gratuities, or other items of value they receive and shall provide a full report of the circumstances of their receipt if directed.**
Scenario 3	At 2 A.M. a police officer, who is on duty, is driving his patrol car on a deserted road. The officer sees a vehicle that has been driven off the road and is stuck in a ditch. The officer approaches the vehicle and observes that the driver is not hurt

	but is obviously intoxicated. The officer also finds that the driver is a police officer. Instead of reporting this accident and offense the officer transports the driver to his home. **IV. A. 8 (b) Officers shall not use their authority or position for financial gain, for obtaining or granting privileges or favors not otherwise available to them or others except as a private citizen, to avoid the consequences of illegal acts for themselves or for others, to barter, solicit, or accept any goods or services whether for the officer or for another.**
Scenario 4	A police officer on foot patrol surprises a man who is attempting to break into an automobile. The man flees. The officer chases him for about two blocks before apprehending him by tackling him and wrestling him to the ground. After he is under control the officer punches him a couple of times in the stomach as punishment for fleeing. **IV. A. 5 (c) While recognizing the need to demonstrate authority and control over criminal suspects and prisoners, officers shall adhere to this agency's use-of-force policy and shall observe the civil rights and protect the well-being of those in their charge.**
Scenario 5	A police officer discovers a burglary of a jewelry shop. The display cases are smashed and it is obvious that many items have been taken. While searching the shop, the takes a watch, worth about two days pay for that officer. The officer reports that the watch had been stolen during the burglary. **IV. A. 1 (a) Officers shall not violate any law or any agency policy, rule or procedure.** **IV. A. 8 (c) Officers shall not purchase, convert to their own use, or have any claim to any found, impounded, abandoned, or recovered property, or any property held or released as evidence.**

IACP National Law Enforcement Standards for the Scenarios

Scenario 6	While on-duty, A police officer finds a wallet in a parking lot. It contains the amount of money equivalent to a full-day's pay for that officer. The officer reports the wallet as lost property, but keeps the money for himself. **IV. A. 8 (c) Officers shall not purchase, convert to their own use, or have any claim to any found, impounded, abandoned, or recovered property, or any property held or released as evidence.**

References

Ajzen, I., & Fishbein, M. (1977). Attitude-behavior relations: A theoretical analysis and review of empirical research. *Psychological Bulletin, 84*(5), 888-918.

Ajzen, I., & Fishbein, M. (1980). *Understanding attitudes and predicting social behavior*. Englewood Cliffs, NJ: Prentice-Hall, Inc.

Akers, R. L. (1985). *Deviant behavior: A social learning approach* (3rd ed.). Belmont, CA: Wadsworth.

Akers, R. L. (1996). Is differential association/social learning cultural deviance theory? Criminology, 34(2), 229-247.

Akers, R. L. (2001). Social learning theory. In Paternoster, R., & Bachman, R. (Eds). Explaining criminals and crime. Los Angeles, CA: Roxbury Publishing Company.

Akers, R. L., & Sellers, C. S. (2004). *Criminological theories: Introduction, evaluation, and application* (4th ed.). Los Angeles: Roxbury.

Albanese, J. S. (2008). *Professional ethics in criminal justice: Being ethical when no one is looking* (2nd ed.). Boston, MA: Pearson Allyn & Bacon.

Anderson, L. M., & Bateman, T. S. (1997). Cynicism in the workplace: Some causes and effects. Journal of Organizational Behavior, 18, 449-469.

Alpert, G. P., & Dunham, R. G. (1997). *Policing urban America*. IL: Waveland Press.

Babbie, E. R. (2001). *The practice of social research* (9th ed.). Belmont, CA: Wadsworth Thomson Learning Inc.

Babbie, E. R., & Maxfield, M. G. (2005). *Research methods for criminal justice and criminology* (4th ed.). Belmont, CA: Wadsworth Thomson Learning Inc.

Bachman, R., & Paternoster, R. (2004). *Statistics for criminology and criminal justice* (2nd ed.). Boston, MA: McGraw-Hill.

Bachman, R., & Schutt, R. K. (2007). The practice of research in criminology and criminal justice (3rd ed.). Thousand Oaks, CA: Pine Forge Press.
Bandura, A. (1969). Principles of behavior modification. New York, NY: Holt, Rinehart, and Winston.
Banks, C. (2004). Criminal justice ethics: Theory and practice. Thousand Oaks, CA: Sage.
Barker, T. (1977). Peer group support for police occupational deviance. Criminology, 15(3), 353-367.
Barker, T. (1978). An empirical study of police deviance other than corruption. Journal of Police Science and Administration, 6, 264-272.
Barker, T. (2006). Police ethics: Crisis in law enforcement. Springfield, IL: Charles Thomas.
Barker, T., & Carter, D. L. (1994). Police deviance (3rd ed.). Cincinnati, OH: Anderson Publishing.
Barker, T., & Roeback, J.B. (1974). A typology of police corruption. Social Problems, 21 (3), 423-479.
Barnett, T. (1992). A preliminary investigation of the relationship between selected organizational characteristics and external whistle-blowing by employees. Journal of Business Ethics, 11, 949-959.
Barnett, T. (2001). Dimensions of moral intensity and ethical decision making: An empirical study. Journal of Applied Social Psychology, 31(5), 1038-1057.
Barnett, T., Bass, K., & Brown, G. (1996). Religiosity, ethical ideology, and intentions to report a peer's wrongdoing. Journal of Business Ethics, 15(11), 1161-1174.
Barnett, T., Cochran, D., & Taylor, G. S (1993). The internal disclosure policies of private-sector employers: An initial look at their relationship to employee whistle-blowing. Journal of Business Ethics, 12(2), 127-136.
Barnett, T., & Valentine, S. (2004). Issue contingencies and marketers' recognition of ethical issues, ethical judgments, and behavioral intentions. Journal of Business Research, 57, 338-346.
Bartels, L. K., Harrick, E., Martell, K., & Strickland, D. (1998). The relationship between ethical climate and ethical problems within human resource management. Journal of Business Ethics, 17(7), 799-804.
Bass, K., Barnett, T., & Brown, G. (1998). The moral philosophy of sales managers and its influence on ethical decision making. The Journal of Personal Selling and Sales Management, 18(2), 1-17.
Baumhart, R. (1961). How ethical are businessmen? Harvard Business Review, 39(4), 6-19.

References

Beams, J. D., Brown, R. M., & Killough, L. N. (2003). An experiment testing the determinants of non-compliance with insider trading laws. Journal of Business Ethics, 45(4), 309-323.

Beck L., & Ajzen, I. (1991). Predicting dishonest actions using the theory of planned behavior. Journal of Research in Personality, 25, 285-301.

Bennett, R. R., & Schimitt, E. L. (2002). The effect of work environment on levels of police cynicism: A comparative study. Police Quarterly, 5(4), 493-522.

Blasi, A. (1980) Bridging moral cognition and moral action: A critical review of the literature. Psychological Bulletin, 88, 1-45.

Borkowski, S. C., & Ugras, T. J. (1998). Business students and ethics: A meta-analysis. Journal of Business Ethics, 17(11), 1117-1127.

Brady, F. N., & Wheeler, G. E. (1996). An empirical study of ethical predispositions. Journal of Business Ethics, 15, 927-940.

Braswell, M. (2005). Ethics, crime, and justice: An introductory note to students. In Braswell, M., McCarthy, B., & McCharty, B. (Eds.). (2005). Justice Crime and Ethics. Cincinnati, OH: Anderson.

Braswell, C. M., & Miller, S. L. (1992). Police Perceptions of ethical decision making: The ideal vs. the real. American Journal of Police, 11(4), 27-45.

Brewer, G. A., & Selden, S. C. (1995). Whistle blowers in the federal civil service: New evidence of the public service ethics? Revised version of paper presented at the annual meeting of the American Political Science Association, Chicago, IL.

Bruce, W. (1994). Ethical people are productive people. Public Productivity & Management Review, 17(3), 241-252.

Burgess, R., & Akers, R. L. (1966). A differential association-reinforcement theory of criminal behavior. Social Problems, 14, 363-383.

Butterfield, K. D., Trevino L. K., & Weaver, G. R. (2000). Moral awareness in business organizations: Influences of issue-related and social context factors. Human Relations, 53(7), 981-1018.

Caldero, M. A., & Crank J. P. (2004). Police ethics: The corruption of noble cause (2nd ed.). Cincinnati, OH: Anderson Publishing.

Carlson, D.S., Kacmar, K. M., & Wadsworth, L. L. (2002). The impact of moral intensity dimensions on ethical decision making: Assessing the relevance of orientation. Journal of Managerial Issues, 14(1), 15-30.

Carmines, E. G., & Zeller, R. A. (1979). Reliability and validity assessment. Beverly Hills, CA: Sage.

Cavanagh, G.F., & Fritzsche, D. (1985). Using vignettes in business ethics research. Research in Corporate Social Performance and Policy, 7, 279-293.

Cavanagh, G.F., Moberg, D.J., & Velasquez, M. (1981). The ethics of organizational politics. Academy of Management Review, 6(3), 363-374.

Chappell, A. T., & Piquero, A. R. (2004). Applying social learning theory to police misconduct. Deviant Behavior, 25, 89-108.

Cherry, J., & Fraedrich, J. (2002). Perceived risk, moral philosophy and marketing ethics: mediating influences on sales managers' ethical decision-making. Journal of Business Research, 55, 951-962.

Chia, A., & Mee, L.S. (2000). The effects of issue characteristics on the recognition of moral issues. Journal of Business Ethics, 27, 255-259.

Cohen, J. (1988). Statistical power analysis for the behavioral sciences (2nd ed.).Hillsdale, NJ: Erlbaum.

Cohen, J. (1992). A power primer. American Psychologist, 112, 155-159.

Cornish, D., & Clarke, R. (1987). Understanding crime displacement: An application of rational choice theory. Criminology, 25(4), 933-947.

Crank, J. P. (1998). Understanding police culture. Cincinnati, OH: Anderson.

Cronbach, L. J. (1951). Coefficient alpha and the internal structure of tests. Psychometrika, 16(3), 297-334.

Cullen, J. B., Victor, B., & Bronson, J. W. (1993). The ethical climate questionnaire: An assessment of its development and validity. Psychological Reports, 73(2), 667-675.

Davidson, R. (2000, March 19). Police corruption scandal may cost Los Angeles more than $200m: [3 Edition]. Sunday Herald, p. 16. Retrieved November 20, 2008, from ProQuest Newsstand database. (Document ID: 72528253).

Davis (1998). Do cops really need a code of ethics? In Braswell, M., McCarthy, B., & McCharty, B. (Eds.). (1998). Justice Crime and Ethics. Cincinnati, OH: Anderson Publishing.

Dawson, L. M. (1992). Will feminization change the ethics of the sales profession? Journal of Personal Selling and Sales Management, 12(1), 21-32.

DeConinck, J. B., & Lewis, W. F. (1997). The influence of deontological and teleological considerations and ethical climate on sales managers' intentions to reward or punish sales force behavior. Journal of Business Ethics, 16(5), 497-506.

Delattre, E. J. (2006). Character and cops: Ethics in policing (5th ed.). Washington, DC: AEI Press.

Detert, J. R., Trevino, L. K., & Sweitzer, V. L. (2008). Moral disengagement in ethical decision making: A study of antecedents and outcomes. Journal of Applied Psychology, 93(2), 374-391.

DeVellis, R. F. (2003). Scale development: Theory and applications. Thousand Oak, CA: Sage.

Dillman, A. D. (2007). Mail and internet surveys: The tailored design method. Hoboken, NJ: John Wiley & Sons.

Dozier, J. B., & Miceli, M. P. (1985). Potential predictors of whistle-blowing: A pro-social behavior perspective. Academy of Management Review, 10(4), 823-836.

Dubinsky, A. J., & Ingram, T. N. (1984). Correlates of salespeople's ethical conflict: An exploratory investigation. Journal of Business Ethics, 3, 343-353.

Dubinsky, A. J., & Levy, M. (1985). Ethics in retailing perceptions of retail salespeople. Journal of the Academy of Marketing Science, 13(1), 1-16.

Dubinsky, A. J., & Loken, B. (1989). Analyzing ethical decision making in marketing. Journal of Business Research, 19(2), 83-107.

Durkheim, E. (2006). Suicide. (Robin Buss, Trans.). New York, NY: Penguin Books. (Original work published 1893).

Durkheim, E. (1933). The division of labor in society. (George Simpson, Trans.). New York, NY: Free Press. (Original work published 1897).

Dworkin, T. M., & Baucus, M. S. (1998). Internal vs. external whistleblowers: A comparison of whistle-blowing processes. Journal of Business Ethics, 17(12), 1281-1298.

Ekenvall, B. (2002). Police attitudes towards fellow officers' misconduct: The Swedish case and a comparison with the USA and Croatia. Journal of Scandinavian Studies in Criminology & Crime Prevention, 3(2), 210-232.

Felkenes, G. T. (1984). Attitudes of police officers toward their professional ethics. Journal of Criminal Justice, 12, 211-220.

Felkenes, G. T. (1987). Ethics in the graduate criminal justice curriculum. Teaching philosophy, 10(1), 23-26.

Ferrell, O. C., & Gresham, L. G. (1985). A contingency framework for understanding ethical decision making in marketing. Journal of Marketing, 49, 87-96.

Ferrell, O. C., & Skinner, S. J. (1988). Ethical behavior and bureaucratic structure in marketing research organizations. Journal of Marketing Research 25, 103-109.

Field, A. (2005). Discovering statistics using SPSS (2nd ed.). Thousand Oak, CA: Sage.

Fishbein, M., & Ajzen, I. (1975). Belief, attitude, intentions and behavior: An introduction to the theory and research. Boston, MA: Addison-Wesley.

Fitzgerald, G. (1989). Report of a commission of inquiry pursuant to orders in council. Government Printer, Queensland.

Flannery, B. L., & May, D. R. (2000). Environmental ethical decision making in the U.S. metal-finishing industry. Academy of Management Journal, 43(4), 642-662.

Ford, R., & Richardson, W. (1994). Ethical decision making: A review of the empirical literature. Journal of Business Ethics, 13(3), 205-221.

Forsyth, D. (1980). A taxonomy of ethical ideologies. Journal of Personality and Social Psychology, 39, 175-184.

Fox, J. (1991). Regression diagnostics. Newbury Park, CA: Sage.

Frey, B. F. (2000). The impact of moral intensity on decision making in a business context. Journal of Business Ethics, 26, 181-195.

Fritzsche, D. J. (1988). An examination of marketing ethics: Role of the decision maker, consequences on the decision, management position, and sex of the respondent. Journal of Macro-marketing, 8 (2), 29-39.

Fritzsche, D. J., & Becker, H. (1984) Linking management behavior to ethical philosophy: An empirical investigation. Academy of Management Journal, 27, 166-175.

Gephart, K. J., Harrison, D. A., & Trevino, L. K. (2007). The who, when, and where of unethical choices: A meta-analysis. Academy of Management Proceedings, 1-6.

Gilligan, C. (1982). In a different voice: Psychological theory and women's development. Cambridge, MA: Harvard University Press.

Glass, R. S., & Wood, W. A. (1996). Situational determinants of software piracy: An equity theory perspective. Journal of Business Ethics, 15(11), 1189-1198.

Goldstein, H. (1975). Police corruption: A perspective on its nature and control. Washington, DC: Police Foundation.

Gold, J. (2005). Utilitarian and deontological approaches to criminal justice. In Braswell, M., McCarthy, B., & McCharty, B. (Eds.). (2005). Justice Crime and Ethics. Cincinnati: Anderson.

Graham, J. W. (1986). Principled organization dissent: A theoretical essay. In Cummings, L. L., & Staw, B. M. (Eds). Research in organizational behavior. Greenwich, CT: JAI Press.

Graham, J. W. (1989). Whistle blowing as organizational citizenship behavior and/or civic duty. Paper presented at the annual meeting of the American Society of Criminology, Reno, NV.

References

Green, D. (1989). Measures of illegal behavior in individual-level deterrence research. Journal of Research in Crime and Delinquency, 26, 253-275.

Greene, J.R., Piquero, A.R., Hickman, M. J., & Lawton, B. A. (2004). Police integrity and accountability in Philadelphia: Predicting and assessing police misconduct. Washington, DC: National Institute of Justice/NCJRS.

Grover, S. L., & Hui, C. (1994). The influence of role conflict and self-interest on lying in organizations. Journal of Business Ethics, 13(4), 295-303.

Haines, R., Street, M. D., & Haines, D. (2007). The influence of perceived importance of an ethical issue on moral judgment, moral obligation, and moral intent. Journal of Business Ethics, 81(2), 387-399.

Haney, C., Banks, C., & Zimbardo, P. (1973). Interpersonal dynamics in a simulated prison. International Journal of Criminology and Penology, 1, 69-97.

Harrington, S. J. (1997). A test of a person-issue contingent model of ethical decision making in organizations. Journal of Business Ethics, 16(4), 363-375.

Hegarty, W., & Sims H. P. Jr. (1978). Some determinants of unethical decision behavior: An experiment. Journal of Applied Psychology, 63(4), 451-457.

Hickman, M. J. (2005) Self-reported and official police problem behavior: Identifying the roles of context, individual, and data. Retrieved from Dissertations & Theses: Full Text database. (AAT 3178786).

Hickman, M.J., Piquero, A. R., Lawton, B. A., Greene, J. R. (2001). Applying Tittle's control balance theory to police deviance. Policing, 24(4), 497-519.

Hickman, M., Piquero, N., & Piquero, A. (2004). The validity of Niederhoffer's cynicism scale. Journal of Criminal Justice, 32(1), 1-13.

Huberts, L., Lamboo, T., Punch, M. (2003). Police integrity in the Netherlands and the United States: Awareness and alertness. Police Practice & Research, 4(3), 217-232.

Hunt, T. G., & Jennings, D. F. (1997). Ethics and performance: A simulation analysis of team decision making. Journal of Business Ethics, 16(2), 195-203.

Hunt, S. D., Kiecker, P. L., & Chonko, L. B. (1990). Social responsibility and personal success: A research note. Journal of the Academy of Marketing Science, 18(3), 239-244.

Hunt, S. D., & Vitell, S. J. (1986). A General Theory of Marketing Ethics. Journal of Macro-marketing, 48, 30-42.

Hyams, M. T. (1990). The relationship of role perception and narcissism to attitudes toward professional ethical behavior among police officers. Ph.D. dissertation. Retrieved November 29, 2008, from Dissertations & Theses: Full Text database. (AAT 9020884).

Ivkovic, K. S. (2003). Measuring police corruption. Journal of Criminal Law and Criminology, 93, 593-649.

Ivkovic, K. S. (2005). Police (mis)behavior: A cross-cultural study of corruption seriousness. An International Journal of Police Strategies & Management, 28(3), 546-566.

Izraeli, D. (1988). Ethical beliefs and behavior among managers: A cross-cultural perspective. Journal of Business Ethics, 7(4), 263-271.

Johnson, A. L. (2007) Organizational cynicism and occupational stress in police officers. Ph.D. dissertation. Retrieved from Dissertations & Theses: Full Text database. (AAT 3302892).

Jones, T. M. (1991). Ethical decision making by individuals in organizations: An issue-contingent model. Academy of Management Review, 16(2), 366-395.

Jones, G. E., & Kavanagh, M. J. (1996). An experimental examination of the effects of individual and situational factors on unethical behavioral intentions in the workplace. Journal of Business Ethics, 15(5), 511-523.

Jones, T. M., & Ryan, L. V. (1997). The link between ethical judgment and action in organizations: A moral approbation approach. Organization Science, 8(6), 663-680.

Jos, P. H., Tompkins, M. E., &. Hays, S. W. (1989). In praise of difficult people: A portrait of the committed whistleblower. Public Administration Review, 49, 552-561.

Kant, I. (1964). Groundwork of the metaphysics of morals (translated by H. J. Paton). New York, NY: Harper & Row.

Kaplan, A. (1964). The conduct of inquiry. San Francisco, CA: Chandler.

Kardasz, F. (2005) Ethics training for law enforcement: A study of current practices. Ed.D. dissertation. Retrieved November 15, 2007, from ProQuest Digital Dissertations database. (AAT 3194848).

Kaye, B. (1992). Codes of ethics in Australian business corporations. Journal of Business Ethics, 11(11), 857-862.

Keenan, J. P., & Sims, R. L. (1995). The organizational and intrapersonal influences on whistle-blowing. Paper submitted to the Social Issues in Management division of the Academy of Management.

References

King III, G., & Hermodson, A. (2000). Peer reporting of coworker wrongdoing: A qualitative analysis of observer attitudes in the decision to report versus not report unethical behavior. Journal of Applied Communication Research, 28(4), 309-329.

King, P. M., & Mayhew, M. J. (2002). Moral judgment development in higher education: Insights from the Defining Issues Test. Journal of Moral Education, 31(3), 247-270.

Kleinig, J. (1996). The ethics of policing. New York: Cambridge University Press.

Kleinig, J. (2008). Ethics and criminal justice: An introduction. Cambridge, UK: Cambridge University Press.

Klockars, B. C., Haberfeld, R. M., & Ivkovic, K. S. (Eds). (2004). The counters of police integrity. Thousand Oaks, CA: Sage.

Klockars, B. C., Ivkovic, K. S., Haberfeld, R. M., & Harver, E. W. (2000). The measurement of police integrity. Washington, DC: U.S. National Institute of Justice.

Knapp, W. (1973). Report of the commission to investigate allegations of police corruption and the city's anti-corruption procedures. George Braziller, New York.

Kohlberg, L. (1958). The development of modes of moral thinking and choice in the years 10 to 16. Ph.D. dissertation. Retrieved October 26, 2008, from Dissertations & Theses: Full Text database. (AAT T-04397).

Kohlberg, L. (1969). Stage and sequence: The cognitive development approach to socialization. In D. Goslin (Ed.), Handbook of socialization theory and research (pp. 347-480). Chicago, IL: Rand McNally.

Krebs, D., Denton, K., & Wark, G. (1997). The forms and functions of real-life moral decision-making. Journal of Moral Education, 26(2), 131-143.

Krejei, P., Kvapil, J., & Semrad, J. (1996). The relation between job satisfaction, job frustration, and narcissism and attitudes toward professional ethical behavior among police officers. In M. Pagon (ed.), Policing in central and Eastern Europe. College of Police and Security Studies, Slovenia.

Laczniak, G., & Inderrieden. E. J. (1987). The influence of stated organizational concern upon ethical decision making. Journal of Business Ethics, 6(4), 297-307.

Leitsch, D. L. (2006). Using dimensions of moral intensity to predict ethical decision-making in accounting. Accounting Education, 15(2), 135-149.

Lewis-Beck, M. S. (1980). Applied regression. Beverly Hills, CA: Sage.

Loe, T. W., Ferrell, L., & Mansfield, P. (2000). A review of empirical studies assessing ethical decision making in business. Journal of Business Ethics, 25, 185-204.

Lotz, R., & Regoli, R. (1977). Police cynicism and professionalism. Human Relations, 30(2), 175-186.

May, D. R., & Pauli, K. P. (2002). The role of moral intensity in ethical decision making. Business & Society, 41(1), 84-117.

Mayo, M. A., & Marks, L. J. (1990). An empirical investigation of a general theory of marketing ethics. Journal of the Academy of Marketing Science, 18, 163-171.

McCabe, D., Butterfield, K., & Trevino, L. (2006). Academic dishonesty in graduate business programs: Prevalence, causes, and proposed action. Academy of Management Learning & Education, 5(3), 294-305.

McCabe, D. L., & Trevino, L. K. (1993). Academic dishonesty: Honor codes and other contextual influences. Journal of Higher Education, 64, 522-538.

McCabe, D. L., Trevino L. K., & Butterfield, K. D. (1996). The influence of collegiate and corporate codes of conduct on ethics-related behavior in the workplace. Business Ethics Quarterly, 6(4), 461-476.

Menard, S. (2002). Longitudinal research. Thousand Oaks, CA: Sage.

Mertler, C. A., & Vannatta, R. A. (2005). Advanced and multivariate statistical methods: Practical application and interpretation. Glendale, CA: Pyrczak Publishing.

Merton, R. K. (1938). Social structure and anomie. American Sociological Review, 3, 672-682.

Mesmer-Magnus, J. R., & Viswesvaran, C. (2005). Whistle-blowing in organizations: An examination of correlates of whistle-blowing intentions, actions, and retaliation. Journal of Business Ethics, 62, 277-297.

Miceli, M. P., Dozier, J. B., & Near, J. P. (1991). Blowing the whistle on data-fudging: A controlled field experiment. Journal of Applied Social Psychology, 21, 301-325.

Miceli, M. P., & Near, J. P. (1984). The relationship among beliefs, organizational position, and whistle-blowing: A discriminant analysis. Academy of Management Journal, 27, 687-705.

Miceli, M. P., & Near, J. P. (1985). Characteristics of organizational climate and perceived wrongdoing associated with whistle-blowing decisions. Personnel Psychology, 48, 525-543.

Miceli, M. P., & Near, J. P. (1988). Individual and situational correlates of whistle-blowing. Personnel Psychology, 41, 267-281.

References

Miceli, M. P., & Near, J. P. (1992). Blowing the whistle: The organizational and legal implications for companies and employees. New York: Lexington Books.

Miceli, M. P., Near, J. P., & Schewenk, C. R. (1991). Who blows the whistle and why? Industrial and Labor Relations Review, 45, 113-130.

Mill, J.S. (1979). Utilitarianism. Indianapolis, IN: Hackett.

Mollen, M. (1994). Report of the commission to investigate allegations of police corruption and the anti-corruption procedures of the police department. The City of New York, New York.

Monahan, G. M., Jr. (1977) Cynicism in the Allentown police department. Pennsylvania: A replication of the Niederhoffer New York study. Retrieved from Dissertations & Theses: Full Text database. (AAT EP21638).

Morgan, A. G., Leech, N. L., Gloeckner, G. W., & Barret, K. C. (2007). SPSS for introductory statistics (3rd ed.). Mahwah, NJ: Lawrence Erlbaum Associates.

Morgan, R. B. (1993). Self and co-worker perceptions of ethics and their relationships to leadership and salary. Academy of Management Journal, 36(1), 200-214.

Morris, S. A., & McDonald, R. A. (1995). The role of moral intensity in moral judgments: An empirical investigation. Journal of Business Ethics, 43, 157-168.

Morris, S.A., Rehbein, K. A., Hosselni, J.C., & Armacost, R. L. (1995). A test of environmental, situational, and personal influences on the ethical intentions of CEOs. Business & Society, 34(2), 119-146.

Niederhoffer, A. (1967). Behind the shield: The police in urban society. Garden City, NY: Doubleday.

O' Fallon, M. J., & Butterfield, K. D. (2005). A review of the empirical ethical decision-making literature: 1996-2003. Journal of Business Ethics, 59(4), 375-413.

Pallant, J. (2005). SPSS survival manual (3rd ed.). New York, McGraw-Hill.

Paolillo, J. G. P., & Vitell, S. J. (2002). An empirical investigation of the influence of selected personal, organizational and moral intensity factors on ethical decision making. Journal of Business Ethics, 35(1), 65-74.

Parmerlee, M. A., Near, J. P., & Jensen, T. C. (1982). Correlates of whistleblower's perceptions of organizational retaliation. Administrative Science Quarterly, 27, 17-34.

Patten, M.L. (2002). Proposing empirical research: A guide to the fundamentals (2nd ed.). Los Angeles, CA: Pyrczak Publishing.

Piaget, J. (1932). The moral judgment of the child. New York: Free Press.

Piquero, A., & Hickman, M. (1999). An empirical test of Tittle's control balance theory. Criminology, 37, 319-341.

Pollock, J. (1998). Ethics in crime and justice (3rd ed.). New York: Wadsworth.

Pollock, J. (2007). Ethical dilemmas and decision making in criminal justice. Belmont: Wadsworth.

Punch, K. F. (2005). Introduction to social research: Quantitative and qualitative approaches (2nd ed.). Thousand Oaks, CA: Sage.

Punch, M. (1985). Conduct unbecoming: The social construction of police deviance and control. New York, NY: Tavistock Publications,

Punch, M. (2003). Rotten orchards: "Pestilence," police misconduct and system failure. Policing and Society, 13(2), 171-196.

Rafky, D. M. (1975). Police cynicism reconsidered: An application of smallest space analysis. Criminology, 13, 168-192.

Raines, J. B. (2006) Ethics, integrity, and police misconduct: Analyzing ethical awareness, standards, and action of law enforcement officers in the United States. Ph.D. dissertation. Retrieved December 5, 2007, from ProQuest Digital Dissertations database. (AAT 3232716).

Randall, D. M., & Fernandes, M.F. (1991). The social desirability response bias in ethics research. Journal of Business Ethics, 10, 805-817.

Raymond, C., & Terrance, J. (2004). Police ethics: Organizational implications. Public Integrity, 7(1), 67-79.

Regoli, R. (1976a). An empirical assessment of Niederhoffer's police cynicism scale. Journal of Criminal Justice, 4, 231-241.

Regoli, R. (1976b). The effects of college education on the maintenance of police cynicism. Journal of Police Science & Administration, 4(3), 340-345.

Regoli, R., Crank, J., & Culbertson, R. (1989). Police cynicism, job satisfaction, and work relations of police chiefs: An assessment of the influence of department size. Sociological Focus, 22(3), 161-171.

Regoli, R., & Crank, J., & Rivera, G. F. (1990). The construction and implementation of an alternative measure of police cynicism. Criminal Justice & Behavior, 17(4), 395-409.

Regoli, R., & Poole, E. (1978). Explaining cynicism among city and county police. Criminal Justice Review, 3(1), 93-99.

Regoli, R., & Poole, E. (1979). Measurement of police cynicism: A factor scaling approach. Journal of Criminal Justice, 7, 37-51.

Reidenbach, R. E., & Robin, D. P. (1988). Some initial steps toward improving the measurements of ethical evaluations of marketing activities. Journal of Business Ethics, 7, 871-879.

Reidenbach, R. E., & Robin, D. P. (1990). A partial testing of the contingency framework for ethical decision making: A path analytical approach. Southern Marketing Association Proceedings, 121–128.

Rest, J. R. (1984). Research on moral development: Implications for training counseling psychologists. Counseling Psychologist, 12(3), 19-29.

Rest, J. R. (1986). Moral development: Advances in research and theory. New York: Praeger.

Rest, J. R., & Narvaez, D. (Eds). (1994). Moral development in the professions: Psychology and applied ethics. Hillsdale, NJ: Lawrence Erlbaum Associates.

Rest, J. R., Narvaaez, D., Bebeau, M. J., & Thoma, S. J. (1999). Postconventional moral thinking: A neo-Kohlbergian approach. Mahwah, NJ: Lawrence Erlbaum Associates.

Robin, D. P., Reidenbach, R. E., & Forrest, P. J. (1996). The perceived importance of an ethical issue as an influence on the ethical decision-making of ad managers. Journal of Business Research, 35, 17–28.

Rokeach, M. (1973). The nature of human values. New York, NY: The Free Press.

Rokeach, M., Miller, M., & Synder, J. (1971). The value gap between police and policed. Journal of Social Issues, 27(2), 155-171.

Ross, W. T., & Robertson, D. C. (2003). A typology of situational factors: Impact on salesperson decision-making about ethical issues. Journal of Business Ethics, 46(3), 213-234.

Rothschild, J., & Miethe, T. (1999). Whistle-Blower disclosures and management retaliation. Work & Occupations, 26(1), 107-128.

Rothwell, G. R. (2003). The code of silence and whistle-blowing in police and civilian public agencies in the state of Georgia. Ph.D. dissertation. Retrieved November 6, 2008, from Dissertations & Theses: Full Text database. (AAT 3092377).

Rothwell, G. R., & Baldwin, N. J. (2007). Whistle-blowing and the code of silence in police agencies. Crime and Delinquency, 53(4), 605-632.

Ruegger, D., & King, E. W. (1992). A study of the effect of age and gender upon student business ethics. Journal of Business Ethics, 11, 179-186.

Sankaran, S., & Bui, T. (2003). Ethical attitudes among accounting majors: An empirical study. Journal of American Academy of Business, Cambridge 3, 71-77.

Shadish, W. R., Cook, T. D., & Campbell, T. D. (2002). Experimental and quasi- experimental designs. Boston: Houghton Mifflin Company.

Shapeero, M., Koh, H. C., & Killough, L. N. (2003). Underreporting and premature sign-off in public accounting. Managerial Auditing Journal, 18, 478-489.

Sherman, L. W. (1978). Scandal and reform: Controlling police corruption. California: University of California Press.

Sherman, L. W. (1982). Learning police ethics. Criminal Justice Ethics, 1(1), 10-19.

Sherman, L. W. (1985). Equity against truth: Value choices in deceptive investigations. In Heffernan, W., & Stroup, T. (Eds) Police ethics: Hard choices in law enforcement. New York: John Jay Press.

Simon, H. (1957). Administrative behavior: A study of decision-making processes in administrative organization (2nd ed.). Oxford England: Macmillan.

Sims, R. L. & Keenan, J. P. (1998). Predictors of external whistle-blowing: Organizational and intrapersonal variables. Journal of Business Ethics, 17, 411-421.

Singer, M. S. (1996). The role of moral intensity and fairness perception in judgments of ethicality: A comparison of managerial professionals and the general public. Journal of Business Ethics, 15(4), 469-474.

Singer, M., Mitchell, S., & Turner, J. (1998). Consideration of moral intensity in ethicality judgments: Its relationship with whistle-blowing and the need for cognition. Journal of Business Ethics, 17, 527-541.

Singhapakdi, A., Salyachivin, S., Virakul, B., & Veerayangkur, V. (2000). Some important factors underlying ethical decision making of managers in Thailand. Journal of Business Ethics, 27(3), 271-284.

Singhapakdi, A., & Vitell, S. J. (1990). Marketing ethics: Factors influencing perceptions of ethical problems and alternatives. Journal of Macromarketing, 10, 4-18.

Singhapakdi, A., Vitell, S. J., & Kraft, K. L. (1996). Moral intensity and ethical decision-making of marketing professionals. Journal of Business Research, 36(3), 245-255.

Skinner, S. J., Ferrell, O. C., & Dubinsky, A. J. (1988). Organizational dimensions of marketing research ethics. Journal of Business Research, 16(2), 209-223.

Skinner, B. F. (1953). Science and human behavior. New York, NY: Macmillan.

References

Skolnick. H. J. (2002). Corruption and the blue code of silence. Police Practice and Research, 3(1), 7-19.

Snizek, W. (1972). Hall's professionalism scale: An empirical assessment. American Sociological Review, 37, 109-114.

Souryal, S. S. (2007). Ethics in criminal justice: In search of the truth (4th ed.). Cincinnati, OH: Anderson Publication.

Soutar, G., M., McNeil, M., & Molster, C. (1994). The impact of the work environment on ethical decision making: Some Australian evidence. Journal of Business Ethics, 13 (5), 327-339.

Stevens, J. (1992). Applied multivariate statistics for the social sciences (2nd ed.). Hillsdale, NJ: Lawrence Erlbaum Associates.

Sutherland, E. H. (1947). Principles of criminology (4th ed.). Philadelphia: J.B. Lippincott.

Sparks, J. R., & Hunt, S. D. (1998). Marketing researcher ethical sensitivity: Conceptualization, measurement, and exploratory investigation. Journal of Marketing, 62(2), 92-109.

Staub, E. (1978). Positive social behavior and morality: Social and personal influences. New York: Academic Press.

Tabachnick, B. G., & Fidell, L. S. (2007). Using multivariate statistics (5th ed.). New York: Harper Collins College Publishers.

Tarde, G. (1912). Penal philosophy. Translated by R. Howell. Boston, MA: Little, Brown.

Taylor, P. W. (1975). Principles of ethics: An introduction. Encino, CA: Dickensen Publishing.

Tenbrunsel, A. E. (1998). Misrepresentation and expectations of misrepresentation in an ethical dilemma: The role of incentives and temptation. *Academy of Management Journal, 41*(3), 330-339.

Trevino, L. K. (1986). Ethical decision making in organizations: A person-situation interactionist model. Academy of Management Review, 11(3), 601-617.

Trevino, L. K., Butterfield, K. D., & McCabe, D. L. (1998). The ethical context in organizations: Influences on employee attitudes and behaviors. Business Ethics Quarterly, 8(3), 447-476.

Trevino, L. K., & Nelson, A. K. (2004). Managing business ethics (3rd ed.). Hoboken, NJ: John Willey & Sons, Inc.

Trevino, L. K., & Victor, B. (1992). Peer reporting of unethical behavior: A social context perspective. Academy of Management Journal, 35(1), 38-64.

Trevino, L. K., & Weaver, G. R. (2001). Organizational justice and ethics program "follow- through": Influences on employees' harmful and helpful behavior. Business Ethics Quarterly, 11(4), 651-671.

Trevino, L. K., & Weaver, G. R. (2003). Managing ethics in business organizations: Social Scientific Perspectives. Stanford, CA: Stanford Business Books.

Trevino, L. K., Weaver, G., & Reynolds, S. (2006). Behavioral ethics in organizations: A review. Journal of Management, 32(6), 951-990.

Trevino, L. K., & Youngblood, S. A. (1990). Bad apples in bad barrels: A causal analysis of ethical decision making behavior. Journal of Applied Psychology, 75(4), 378-385.

United States General Accounting Office. (1998). Information on drug related police corruption. Washington, DC: U.S. Government Printing Office.

Victor, B., & Cullen, J. B. (1988).The organizational bases of ethical work climates. Administrative Science Quarterly, 33, 101-125.

Victor, B., Trevino, L. K., & Shapiro, D. (1993). Peer reporting of unethical behavior: The influence of justice evaluations and social context factors. Journal of Business Ethics, 12(4), 253-263.

Vold, G. B., Bernard, T. J., & Snipes, J. B. (2002). Theoretical Criminology. New York, NY: Oxford University Press.

Wahn, J. (1993). Organizational dependence and the likelihood of complying with organizational pressures to behave unethically. Journal of Business Ethics, 12(3), 245-251.

Walker, S. (2005). The new world of police accountability. Thousands Oak, CA: Sage.

Warr, M. (2001). The social origins of crime: Edwin Sutherland and the theory of differential association. In Paternoster, R., & Bachman, R. (Eds). Explaining criminals and crime. Los Angeles, CA: Roxbury Publishing Company.

Weaver, K. M., & Ferrell, O. C. (1977). The impact of corporate policy in reported ethical beliefs and behavior of marketing practitioners. AMA Proceedings, 477-481.

Weaver, G. R., & Trevino, L. K. (1999). Compliance and values oriented ethics programs: Influences on employees' attitudes and behavior. Business Ethics Quarterly, 9(2), 315-335.

Weber, J. (1992). Scenarios in business ethics research: Review, critical assessment, and recommendations. Business Ethics Quarterly, 2(2), 137-160.

Weeks, W. A., Moore, C. W., McKinney, J. A., & Longenecker, J. G. (1999). The effects of gender and career stage on ethical judgment. Journal of Business Ethics, 20(4), 301-313.

Weeks, W., & Nantel, J. (1992). Corporate codes of ethics and sales force behavior: A case study. Journal of Business Ethics, 11(10), 753-760.

Westmarland, L. (2005). Police ethics and integrity: Breaking the blue code of silence. Policing and Society, 15(2), 145-165.

Wilson, J. Q., & Kelling, G. L. (1982). Broken windows: The police and neighborhood safety. Atlantic Monthly, 29-38.

Wu, C. (2003). A study of the adjustment of ethical recognition and ethical decision-making of managers- to-be across the Taiwan Strait before and after receiving a business ethics education. Journal of Business Ethics, 45(4), 291-307.

Yetmar, S. A., & Eastman, K. K. (2000). Tax practitioners' ethical sensitivity: A model and empirical examination. Journal of Business Ethics, 26(4), 271-288.

Zabid, A. R. M., & Alsagoff, S. K. (1993). Perceived ethical values of Malaysian managers. Journal of Business Ethics, 12(4), 331-337.

Zey-Ferrell, M., & Ferrell, O. C. (1982). Role-set configuration and opportunity as predictors of unethical behavior in organizations. Human Relations, 35(7), 587-604.

Zey-Ferrell, M., Weaver, K. M., & Ferrell, O. C (1979). Predicting unethical behavior among marketing practitioners. Human Relations, 32(7), 557-569.

Index

Code of Silence, 2, 3, 18, 131, 142, 157, 159, 161
Codes of Ethics, 57, 58
Cognitive Moral Development, 18, 19, 20, 21, 141
Concentration of Effect, 5, 28, 35, 75
Criminal Justice, 5, 48, 134, 145, 149, 150, 153
Cynicism, 6, 15, 33, 44, 45, 46, 47, 48, 49, 50, 51, 52, 53, 54, 66, 82, 83, 84, 92, 95, 96, 97, 98, 102, 103, 104, 114, 115, 120, 121, 122, 124, 127, 130, 131, 135, 147, 151, 152,
Defining Issues Test, 20, 32,153
Demographic Factors, 6, 41
Deontology, 11, 12, 13, 14
Descriptive Ethics, 4, 11, 15, 18
Differential Association, 66
Differential Reinforcement, 65, 67
Dispositional Factors, 6, 26, 33, 60, 81
Ethical Decision Making, 1, 2, 4, 5, 6, 7, 9,10, 15, 17, 18, 21, 22, 23, 24, 25, 26, 27, 28, 29, 30, 31, 32, 33, 34, 35, 37, 38, 40, 41, 44, 53, 54, 55, 56, 57, 59,

62, 63, 64, 66, 67, 68, 69, 70, 72, 73, 74, 75, 76, 78, 79, 81, 87, 88, 89, 93, 95, 99, 100, 127, 128, 129, 131, 133, 135, 136, 137, 139, 141, 142, 146, 147, 149, 150, 151, 153,
Ethical Issue, 3, 9, 27, 28, 100, 114, 127, 133, 151
Ethics, 3, 4, 5, 6, 9, 10, 11, 12, 13, 14, 15, 16, 17, 23, 32, 33, 46, 54, 55, 56, 57, 58, 59, 60, 61, 62, 63, 68, 69, 76, 78, 82, 83, 87, 88, 89, 90, 92, 93, 95, 98, 102, 103, 104, 114, 115, 118, 120, 121, 122, 124, 127, 129, 132, 133, 134, 135, 139, 141, 142, 143, 145, 146, 147, 148, 149, 150, 152, 153
Four Component Model, 1, 4, 18, 21, 22, 23, 24, 26, 29, 39
Issue-Contingent Model, 1, 4, 5, 18, 25, 30, 78, 152
Issue-Related Factors, 6, 7, 25, 29, 35, 38, 78, 81, 82, 84, 89, 124, 127, 142
Magnitude of Consequences, 5, 6, 28, 29, 35, 75, 76, 77, 78, 82, 89, 95

171

Moral Awareness, 21, 23
Moral Behavior, 4, 14, 21, 22, 23, 24, 25, 37, 38, 39, 136
Moral Intensity, 5, 10, 28, 29, 35, 41, 73, 78, 79, 89, 100, 106, 133, 134, 146, 147, 150, 153,
Moral Intent, 4, 7, 14, 21, 22, 23, 35, 37, 38, 93, 136, 151
Moral Issue, 4, 5, 9, 15, 22, 28, 31, 35, 73
Moral Judgment, 4, 19, 20, 21, 22, 23, 25, 26, 32, 151
Moral Reasoning, 19, 20, 21, 23, 30, 135
Morality, 4, 10, 11, 13, 19, 20, 24, 28, 30
Organizational Factors, 6, 27, 29, 33, 34, 49, 60, 64, 67, 81, 82, 95, 106, 124, 127, 133
Peer Reporting, 1, 3, 5, 6, 7, 10, 18, 23, 24, 25, 26, 29, 33, 35, 37, 38, 39, 40, 41, 43, 44, 62, 63, 72, 76, 77, 78, 81, 82, 84, 87, 89, 90, 93, 95, 99, 100, 102, 103, 106, 107, 110, 114, 115, 116, 117, 118, 119, 120, 121, 122, 123, 124, 127, 128, 129, 130, 131, 132, 133, 134, 136, 137, 138, 139, 140, 141, 142, 143, 153

Person-Situation Interactionist Model, 1, 4, 5, 26, 27Police Corruption, 3, 4, 16, 17, 39, 146, 152, 153
Police Officers, 2, 44, 47, 50, 57, 66, 72, 82, 103, 104, 124, 125, 129, 132, 133
Probability of Effect, 5, 28, 35, 74
Proximity, 5, 28, 35
Reliability and Validity, 7, 147
Social Consensus, 5, 6, 28, 29, 35, 74, 75, 78, 79, 82, 95, 100, 102, 103, 106, 107, 114, 115, 120, 124, 133, 134, 142
Social Learning Theory, 67, 72, 145
Teleology, 11, 12, 14
Temporal Immediacy, 5, 28, 35
Unethical Behavior, 1, 2, 3, 10, 16, 19, 21, 34, 35, 37, 38, 39, 40, 41, 54, 55, 56, 62, 63, 64, 65, 67, 68, 70, 71, 72, 77, 81, 82, 99, 106, 133, 137, 138, 139, 140, 142, 143, 153
Unethical Decision, 5, 9, 15, 17, 25, 27, 28, 54, 66, 72, 138, 151
Utilitarianism, 12
Whistle-Blowing, 40, 41, 42, 43, 55, 56, 74, 81, 85, 86, 128, 140, 146, 149, 152